T0153388

"Girondo's poetry is a song to the transgressive imagination, an assault on routine. . . . Unlike other experimental artists, his gestures usually transcended mere provocation. His work not only paved the way for a rigorous *vanguardia*, with a profound theoretical basis, but it also took up the quotidian as a field of action, enriching it with an absurd humor that ties it to a Hispanic tradition that stretches from Quevedo and Gracián to Ramón Gómez de la Serna, Julio Cortázar, or Augusto Monterroso. Both shores of the language, with their intense cultural differences, are present (and both are parodied) in these poems that are something like scenes of self-criticism."

—Andrés Neuman

"Girondo's effectiveness undeniably frightens me. I came to his work from the suburbs of my own verse, from that long line of mine where there are sunsets and little lanes and a blurry girl who looks clear next to a sky-blue balustrade. I saw him as so skillful, so apt at hopping off a streetcar in full stride, being reborn safe and sound amid the menace of car horns and stepping away from the passing crowd, that I felt provincial next to him. . . . Girondo is a violent one. He looks on things at length and suddenly gives them a smack."

—Jorge Luis Borges

Decals

Complete Early Poems

Oliverio Girondo

Translated from the Spanish
by Rachel Galvin and
Harris Feinsod

Illustrations by
the Author

OPEN LETTER
LITERARY TRANSLATIONS FROM THE UNIVERSITY OF ROCHESTER

Library of Congress Cataloging-in-Publication Data: Available
ISBN-13: 978-1-940953-87-8 / ISBN-10: 1-940953-87-1

*This project is supported in part by the
Alice Kaplan Institute for the Humanities at Northwestern University.*

*This project is supported in part by the New York State Council on the Arts with the
support of Governor Andrew M. Cuomo and the New York State Legislature.*

Printed on acid-free paper in the United States of America.

Text set in Jenson Pro, an old-style serif typeface drawn by Robert Slimbach,
based on a Venetian old-style text face cut by Nicolas Jenson in 1470.

Design by N. J. Furl

Open Letter is the University of Rochester's nonprofit, literary translation press:
Dewey Hall 1-219, Box 278968, Rochester, NY 14627

www.openletterbooks.org

Contents

Introduction vii

Twenty Poems to Be Read on the Streetcar
(1922)

Open Letter to *La Púa* 7

Breton Landscape 13

Café-Concert 17

Sketch in the Sand 19

Nocturne 23

Rio de Janeiro 25

Street Note 29

Milonga 31

Venice 35

Ex-Voto 39

Holiday in Dakar 43

Sevillian Sketch 45

Carnival Parade 49

Biarritz 51

Another Nocturne 55

Pedestrian 57

Chioggia 61

Plaza 65

Lago Maggiore 69

Sevillian 73

Verona 77

Decalcomania
(1925)

Toledo 83

Las Sierpes Street 89

The Express Train 93

Gibraltar 103

Tangier 107

Siesta 117

Carousal 119

Escorial 127

Alhambra 133

Holy Week 139

Acknowledgments 161

INTRODUCTION

Things are never only what they seem in Oliverio Girondo's early poems, and in fact they often merely imitate reality. In "Rio de Janeiro," the city "is a cardboard imitation of a porphyry city," and in "Siesta," Girondo writes, "How real, the landscape that looks fake!" "Café-Concert" ends with the line "The curtain, on closing, simulates a half-open curtain." Land and sea are inclined to mingle. The poems are crisscrossed by the constant embarking and disembarking of ships, often metaphorically, so that elderly women "board" the nave of a church and weary, land-bound sailors "board" the city's cafés. The present moment mixes with memory, and nostalgia is a type of pipe smoke that wafts through the city. Sometimes a tavern is also a bullring, as in "Carousal," where the waiter inserts a corkscrew the way a *picador* jabs a bull with his lance. Everywhere, Girondo conveys the teeming metropolis with striking sensory details and playful comparisons. These lines from "Street Note" aptly summarize this urban experience: "I think about where I will store the kiosks, streetlamps, passersby that enter through my pupils. I feel so full I fear I'll burst . . . I might need to drop some ballast on the walkway." There are fleeting city scenes described as "notes" or "sketches," nocturnes, landscape poems, tango and nightclub poems, travel tales of ethnographic encounter, critiques of Catholic ritual, and a lone, unrhymed sonnet ("Siesta"). In one poem, Girondo announces the "Humble and humiliated song of urinals tired of singing!" in a twist on Marcel Duchamp's famous 1917 provocation. In these poems, the nightingale of lyric is

replaced by a banal object already debased at an early moment of technological modernity. Car horns, shadows, and other elements of the evolving cityscape all take on intense feelings of their own.

This volume brings together the complete texts of the first two poetry collections published by the Argentine poet Oliverio Girondo, *Twenty Poems to Be Read on the Streetcar* (*Veinte poemas para ser leídos en el tranvía*, 1922), and *Decalcomania* (*Calcomanías*, 1925). For the first time in English translation, we present these thirty poems in their original sequence, alongside Girondo's own spirited watercolor illustrations. These books showcase Girondo's central place in the Argentine avant-garde, perhaps second only to his friend and sometime adversary, Jorge Luis Borges. Borges recalled his envy for the metropolitan ease of Girondo's poetry in the 1920s: "I saw him as so skillful, so apt at hopping off a streetcar in full stride, being reborn safe and sound amid the menace of car horns and stepping away from the passing crowd, that I felt provincial next to him."* Borges and Girondo, along with their fellow writers in the famed Florida group of Buenos Aires, all wrote of what it meant to feel modern and worldly. They took cues from the avant-garde movements they observed firsthand or read about in Paris, Milan, Zurich, and Madrid. They joined a company of Latin American writers and artists making an entrance into the global avant-garde, such as Oswald de Andrade and Tarsila do Amaral of Brazil and Vicente Huidobro of Chile (with his one-person movement of "creationism"). The year 1922 alone saw the publication of Peruvian writer César Vallejo's *Trilce*, the establishment of *Estridentismo* in Mexico, the staging of The Modern Art Week in São Paulo, and the appearance of Borges's Ultraist manifesto.

Twenty Poems to Be Read on the Streetcar carves a distinctly Argentine path through the overwhelming experience of worldwide urban modernity, at home in Buenos Aires, Rio de Janeiro, and Dakar, as

---

* Jorge Luis Borges, *El tamaño de mi esperanza* (Buenos Aires: Proa, 1926).

well as tourist hotspots in Western Europe: Douarnenez, Paris, Biarritz, Seville, Lago Maggiore, and Venice. The great Peruvian Marxist critic José Carlos Mariátegui marveled at how Girondo's poems absorbed sights, sounds, and literary techniques from European cities without diminishing his creole identity as a Latin American poet: "The Western metropolis has polished his five or more senses; but it has not slowed or spoiled them." He continues: "In Girondo's poetry, the embroidery is European, urban, cosmopolitan, but the weave is all Gaucho."* When Girondo's friend Evar Méndez asked him for a prologue to the second edition, Girondo wrote an open letter to the culinary magazine *La Púa*, likening this creole cosmopolitanism to an ironclad Latin American stomach: "the best stomach in the world, an eclectic, very free stomach, able to digest, and to digest well, a northern herring or oriental couscous as much as a godwit cooked on an open flame or one of those epic Spanish chorizos." We might compare this to the 1928 "Anthropophagous Manifesto" of Oswald de Andrade, who thought Brazilian culture would flourish thanks to its cannibalistic capacity to digest and re-express cultural imports from Europe.

Twenty Poems offers an exuberant record of cities, cafés, ports of call, and picturesque seaside villages in an age where colonialism mixes overtly with global tourism. In a 1931 author's note, Girondo boasted, "I have lived 567 days at sea," and just so, a lyric sea diary offers some structure to the collection, knitting far-flung city scenes together. However, Girondo re-ordered the poems he composed to create jumps in time and space, rather than a neat chronological sequence.

For readers today, the title *Twenty Poems to Be Read on the Streetcar* may evoke an image of urban flânerie, exactly contemporary to

---

* José Carlos Mariátegui, "Oliverio Girondo," *Variedades* [Lima] (August 15, 1925): 101-103. Qtd. in Oliverio Girondo, *Obra completa*, ed. Raúl Antelo ([San José]: Universidad de Costa Rica, 1999): 615.

Mário de Andrade's *Paulicéia Desvairada* (*Hallucinated City*, 1922), and a halfway mark between Charles Baudelaire's *Les fleurs du mal* (*The Flowers of Evil*, 1857) and Frank O'Hara's **Lunch Poems** (1965). Yet, unlike the City Lights "Pocket Poets" series where O'Hara's volume later appeared, *Twenty Poems to Be Read on the Streetcar* was not actually meant to fit into a back pocket and be perused on a morning commute. In fact, Girondo first published it in France in an oversize, demi-luxe edition, embossed and illustrated with his own watercolors. The idea of reading this particular volume of poems on a streetcar was an elaborate joke, as though such a large book could be casually flipped open while sitting shoulder to shoulder amid the tramway crowd. In 1925, Girondo republished *Twenty Poems* through the editorial house of the avant-garde journal *Martín Fierro*, this time in a cheap paperback "Streetcar Edition."

Between 1923 and 1925, Girondo traveled extensively in Spain and brought out his second book *Decalcomania* in Madrid, a sequence of ten long travel poems of wry observations about Spanish modernization. "Decalcomania" refers to an artistic process by which an image in one medium (such as a print) is transferred onto another medium (such as a ceramic vase or a canvas). The product is now known simply as a "decal." In the 1930s, many surrealist painters experimented with the technique, but a decade earlier Girondo employed the decal as a metaphor for a verbal construct, imagining the poem as a medium onto which the poet's sudden visual impressions are transferred. He observes Spain as a collection of outdated-yet-modern, ironic images that are ready-made to "impress" on the page. The poems can be understood as serialized "decals" of Spain, fantastic luggage stickers or guidebook illustrations, not unlike the sort of poetic implied by the title of Mina Loy's poem "Lunar Baedeker."

Girondo's *Decalcomania* fit into a trend of literature depicting travel to Spain in the 1920s (readers may think of North American works by John Dos Passos, Ernest Hemingway, or Waldo Frank). These

writers romanticized the pre-industrial character of picturesque "Old Spain," sometimes sidestepping mass poverty and growing political instability. Girondo's *Decalcomania* deflates that romance, and in this respect the poems prefigure the Italian scholar Mario Praz's anti-travelogue *Unromantic Spain* (1929), which lampooned North American tourists taking muleback tours to feel the thrill of life before the motorcar. Girondo's poems refuse to celebrate such lethargy. Not even the date Girondo liked to place at the end of each poem can be fixed amid Spain's halting adoption of technological standardization. "Express Train," a poem of exasperation at delayed travel, ends "Spain? 1870? . . . 1923? . . ."

✦

Born into a wealthy family on August 17, 1891 in Buenos Aires, the youngest of five brothers, Girondo saw his childhood home on Lavalle Street demolished in the 1930s for the construction of the grand July 9 Avenue. In life and in literature Girondo would often celebrate the convulsive processes of modernization or mock their failure to materialize. In 1900, at age eight, he accompanied his parents on a visit to attend the Exposition Universelle in Paris. He saw Oscar Wilde pass by with a sunflower in his lapel, the sort of sartorial detail his early poems frequently note. Insatiable for Europe, he returned often in his adolescence, studying at Louis Le Grand in Paris and Epsom College in Surrey, England. He struck a bargain with his parents in 1909: he agreed to study law if they consented to send him to Europe every year. By the mid 1910s, Girondo began frequenting the major literary salons in Buenos Aires. At the Hotel París, he met the *Caras y caretas* (*Faces and Masks*) magazine group and the poet Baldomero Fernández Moreno. In 1918 Girondo traveled again to Europe and Africa, and wrote for *Caras y caretas* about the Argentine Cubo-Futurist painter Emilio Pettoruti, whom he met in Lombardy.

Returning to Buenos Aires, he worked alongside Ricardo Güiraldes and Evar Méndez to reenergize the flagging journal *Proa* (*Prow*), which became an important outlet for his poetry. From April to August 1920 he again journeyed through Europe, composing poems along the way. These were the poems he gathered, in 1922, into *Twenty Poems to Be Read on the Streetcar*. The publication increased his visibility in the emerging vanguard, and when the editor Samuel Glusberg prompted Méndez to found a new journal called *Martín Fierro* (named after a previous magazine, which was in turn named after the outlaw hero of a famous nineteenth-century gaucho poem), Méndez quickly drew Girondo into its orbit. Girondo wrote the group's 1924 manifesto and often filled the columns of the journal with his *Membretes* (*Colophons*). These pithy aphorisms borrow, as do Girondo's poems, from the style of the Spanish Ultraist Ramón Gomez de la Serna's invented genre of *greguerías*, or humorous one-liners. These hinge on a surprising or absurd metaphor, a signature rhetorical device of the Ultraist movement.

Martín Fierro had a nationalist edge to it, but it also imagined a Pan-Latin American and European audience, announcing the arrival of Argentine literature to a world readership.* Girondo turned his cosmopolitan wanderlust into promotional work. In 1924, he traveled widely in Latin America, building a network of literary and intellectual exchange with vanguard groups in Peru, Cuba, and Mexico. He did not shy away from promoting his own works or keeping track of his admirers. Every Spanish critic who wrote a favorable review of *Twenty Poems* earned a dedication in a poem in *Decals*.** The cheap "Streetcar Edition" of *Twenty Poems* was another promotional experiment. Later,

---

* See Beatriz Sarlo, *Modernidad periférica: Buenos Aires 1920 y 1930* (Buenos Aires: Nueva Visión, 1988).

** Trinidad Barrera, "'El gaucho que atrapa a lazo las greguerías criollas.' Oliverio Girondo en España durante la década de los veinte," in Girondo, *Obra Completa*, 449.

with the publication of *Espantapájaros: al alcance de todos* (*Scarecrow: Within the Reach of All*, 1932), Girondo took his publicity stunts to new heights. He sold out the entire run of 5000 copies in under a month by renting a six-horse funeral carriage attended by full livery, which paraded around town carrying a huge, papier-mâché scarecrow in a top hat and monocle. He then rented a shop on calle Florida where attractive young women were hired to sell the book.

In 1926, Girondo met a striking twenty-year-old redhead named Norah Lange, the daughter of Norwegian and Irish immigrants, who was working as a clerk while publishing her first books of poetry. In most accounts, their love for one another came at the chagrin of a heartsick Jorge Luis Borges. The couple, who eventually married in 1943, held court at the center of the Buenos Aires avant-garde through much of the 1920s and 1930s, forging hijinks-fueled friendships with occasional visitors such as Pablo Neruda, Federico García Lorca, and Alfonso Reyes. When Girondo published *Interlunio* in 1937, Lange gave him a kind of public coronation, laureling him in a wreath made of electric lights. She also quipped that Girondo had transformed from playing the role of tireless traveler to that of "insular landowner," since he had purchased a house at calle Suipacha.*

True enough, by the 1940s, his poems shied away from his earlier cosmopolitanism, tending toward a concern with national questions in books like *Persuasión de los días* (*Persuasion of the Days*, 1942) and especially in *Campo Nuestro* (*Our Country*, 1946). The most important work of his late career is *En la masmédula* (1955), a collection of poems that stretch, scatter, and recombine words with evident delight, and which reconfirmed his place in Argentine letters at the leading edge of verbal experimentation. Molly Weigl has wonderfully translated these poems as *In the Moremarrow* (2013).

---

* Norah Lange, "A Oliverio Girondo," in *Estimados congéneres* (Buenos Aires: Losada, 1968). Qtd. in Girondo, *Obra Completa*, 624.

Girondo remained a fixture of Argentine literature until his death in January 1967. By that time, what Pablo Neruda called the "iconoclastic excess" of Girondo's early poems held a distinct place in the story of Latin America's diminishing reliance on European cultural models. Neruda's long elegy "Oliverio Girondo" characterized that story in this way:

> *Se trata del inolvidable.*
> *De su indeleble puntería*
> *cuando borró la catedral*
> *y con su risa de corcel*
> *clausuró el turismo de Europa,*
> *reveló el pánico del queso*
> *frente a la francesa golosa*
> *y dirigió al Guadalquivir*
> *el disparo que merecía.*
>
> *Oh primordial desenfadado!*
> *Hacía tanta falta aquí tu iconoclasta desenfreno!**

> It has to do with the indelible.
> With his unforgettable aim
> when he wiped out the cathedral
> and with his steed-like laugh
> he ended tourism in Europe,
> revealed the cheese's panic
> as it faced the greedy Frenchwoman

---

* Pablo Neruda, "Oliverio Girondo," in *Obras Completas III*, ed. Hernán Loyola (Barcelona: Círculo de Lectores/Galaxia Gutenberg, 2000): 426-429.

and aimed at the Guadalquivir
the shot that it deserved.

Oh essential insouciant one!
How we needed your iconoclastic excess here!

◆

Translators and translations rarely exist in isolation—and this was certainly our experience in collaborating on translating this book. One day in 2012 we fell to conversing about books we wished to teach that had not yet been translated into English. Both of us immediately thought of Girondo's early avant-garde poetry. We were taken with Girondo's vivacity, his wit, and his memorable images. Who can forget the person "crucified" by throwing open a fifth-floor window, the shadow that commits suicide under a streetcar, or the twins fighting it out in the belly of a pregnant woman? Girondo is a major Latin American poet, but he has not been read in North America as frequently as his confrères Borges or Macedonio Fernández. A few poems were translated by a U.S. Naval officer during World War II, and some rendered into English by Molly Weigel and more recently Heather Cleary, but a full translation of Girondo's extraordinary early books of poems has been long overdue. When Rachel said that she was thinking of translating the books, Harris casually revealed that in 2006 he had published two of the *Twenty Poems* translated by his friend Gabriel Milner in a little magazine he was then editing; and that, on something of a lark, they had subsequently worked on a partial draft of the two books, but that it had languished unfinished. As Girondo writes in his *Membretes* (*Colophons*), "There's no critic like a desk drawer."

Struck by this coincidence, we joined forces. Harris sent Rachel the draft, and she began editing, rewriting, annotating, and translating

the remaining poems. In the following years, we collaborated via email and phone calls, and took advantage of any opportunity that brought us to the same city to work on the poems together elbow-to-elbow. Translating was a thoroughly collaborative process. We read the poems aloud in English and Spanish (separately and interlineally) and debated word choices. Our ideas zinged back and forth until it wasn't clear who had come up with which turn of phrase or which solution to a problem. Occasionally, our surroundings contributed to the translation process in a manner we suspected would have amused Girondo—as when some captive flamingos ambled by our table at a restaurant in Las Vegas. It was enormous fun, but we also discovered that translation à deux demands a particular rigor that is a deep form of interpretation: line by line, we explained to one another what we saw in a poem, how we thought an image worked, or what a mysterious phrasing or complicated syntax might signify. We left no linguistic knot undiscussed. And though we entirely transformed the poems during this process, Gabriel Milner's own Girondo-like wit still shines through in many places, such as in "Sketch in the Sand" and the long sequence "Holy Week."

Reading aloud also meant that our shared commitment to the rhythm of the poems remained at center stage. At every turn, we wanted the English versions to have the same elasticity and punch as Girondo's Spanish. His weirdness and wit are inseparable from his soundplay, and we wanted the English to possess a similar euphony and occasional cacophony. His lexicon is idiosyncratic not only because his slang and his terms for technology were au courant one hundred years ago, but also because his Spanish is a decidedly Argentine Spanish. The *lunfardo* or underground Argentine slang of the *milongas* (tango dance events) and *boliches* (night clubs) in some of the poems is quite particular to the time and social spaces of Buenos Aires nightlife. He mentions the *candombé*, a type of African slave music and dance believed to have inspired the tango, and the *bandoneón*, an

instrument of the concertina family that is essential to tango, as well as terms like *jeta*, a slang word for "face" or "mug."

Questions arose. Should we select terms that would have been used in English in the 1920s, to remain close to Girondo's now somewhat anachronistic vocabulary, or choose a contemporary word that would be more recognizable to modern readers? This is a common question in translation and we debated it roundly, generating "Ngram" charts to compare the frequency of certain usages. We often drew on the historical specificity of certain terms—as in the dreadnoughts, frigates, and bunting of maritime transit; the Miura bulls bred for the Spanish bullfight; and the rituals involved in the public celebrations of Catholic holidays.

Some of these poems afford a glimpse of the intense wordplay that would later come to characterize Girondo's poetry in his watershed book *In the Moremarrow*. In "Holy Week," for example, we faced the challenge of translating a pun on *papa* (potato) and *Papa* (pope). We devised a solution by ushering some friars into the scene of preprandial confusion:

> El "menú" nos hace volver en sí. Leemos, nos refregamos los ojos y volvemos a leer:
> "Sopa de Nazarenos".
> "Lenguado a la Pío X".
> —¡Camarero! Un bife con papas.
> —¿Con Papas, señor? . . .
> —¡No, hombre!, con huevos fritos.

> The very "menu" makes us come to. We read, rub our eyes, and read again:
> —Soup of Nazarenes.
> —Sole of Pious X.

"Waiter! I'll have a steak and fries."

"Friars, sir?"

"No man! . . . fried eggs."

We sometimes amplified Girondo's sound play. In stanza two of "Nocturne," for example, we riffed on the repeated plosive "p" sound:

> ¿A qué nos hace recordar el aullido de los gatos en celo, y
> cuál será la intención de los papeles que se arrastran en los
> patios vacíos?

> What does the howl of these cats in heat call to mind,
> and what can the scraps of paper be plotting as they slither
> onto empty patios?

Likewise, in "Ex Voto," we tried to conjure up some sound play that would call back to the flourish we heard in the Spanish:

> Las chicas de Flores, tienen los ojos dulces, como las almen-
> dras azucaradas de la Confitería del Molino, y usan moños
> de seda que les liban las nalgas en un aleteo de mariposa.

> The Flores girls have sweet eyes, like the candied almonds
> at the Confitería El Molino, and they wear silk ribbons
> that sip at their buttocks with the flutter of a butterfly.

At times translating into English meant condensing the Spanish, as in the last line of the poem "Nocturno." We translated "cantar de las canillas mal cerradas" as "leaky faucet song" to maintain the mood while making the phrase compact and contemporary to our ears.

Girondo's idiolect regularly includes French, Italian, and English terms (maquereau, cocotte, pizzicato, campanile, dandys). For the sake of

clarity, we italicized loan-words that have not (yet) been incorporated into the English-language dictionary. Spanish terms that are commonly used in English, such as burro, churros, horchata, and saeta, we did not italicize. It's worth noting that Girondo uses quotation marks liberally, sometimes to indicate place names, foreign imports (such as "chewing gum"), to express irony, or to dramatize a metaphor (as in "Carousal"). We followed English-language conventions at times, but maintained a generous sprinkling of his quotation marks even when they felt superfluous to us. They float around words like fireflies, drawing a winking attention to them.

Even Girondo's punctuation and syntax posed some interesting translation dilemmas. His use of comma splices might sound abrupt, or a prepositional phrase might unfold too leisurely when a pithier English alternative was available. We tried to restrain ourselves from creating a new sentence or using a semicolon instead of Girondo's characteristic comma, choosing to preserve the rhythm of his syntax as best we could.

Some crucial scenes of sexuality and racial difference posed problems we discussed at length. In "Ex Voto," the poet crafts a language of sexual candor that captures new social relations in the city. With dark irony, "Ex Voto" graphically describes the play of gazes upon the female body in the city streets. Young women find that "men's desire suffocates them so much that sometimes they want to shed it like a corset, since they lack the courage to cut their bodies into pieces and toss them to everyone who passes them on the sidewalk." The disassembling of women's bodies plays on the classic poetic device of the blazon, which catalogues a woman's physical attributes, at the same time as it participates in avant-garde habits of fragmentation. Floating heads and amputated legs also appear in poems such as "Sketch in the Sand," but most often, the fragmentation is gendered, as Girondo at once participates in and criticizes the objectifying gaze turned upon the female body.

Whereas Girondo's representations of sex and gender remain ambivalent, mixing progressive critiques with chauvinist fantasies, a few poems include indisputably anti-Semitic and racist tropes. We discovered that in the rich tradition of criticism on Girondo's work, these aspects have not yet received extended commentary. As two Jewish Americans who condemn this language and the attitudes it expresses, we grappled with the decision to expend our energies on translating poems we found repellant, such as "Rio de Janeiro," "Holiday in Dakar," and "Tangier." After much deliberation, we concluded that we would translate all of the poems in both collections. We believe that readers and scholars should be given full access to Girondo's work, in all of its troubling complexity and self-contradictions, rather than conceal racism or bigotry by omission, or simply shut the door on this writer altogether. Girondo's work is an important instance of influential aesthetic achievement that is celebrated despite its entanglement with historical racism.

"Many Argentine poets got their start by reading Girondo," notes Andrés Neuman. "Thus there is nothing more fascinating than rediscovering how Girondo got started with his own poetry." For countless Latin American writers across several generations, his work has been a touchstone. It is our hope that with this translation into English, new generations of readers will be provoked, amused, and galvanized by Girondo's sui generis poetics.

RACHEL GALVIN &
HARRIS FEINSOD
Chicago, July 2018.

Twenty Poems

to be
read on the
streetcar

(1922)

No prejudice is more ridiculous than the prejudice of the SUBLIME

To *La Púa*

Fraternal Cenacle, with the comforting certainty that, in our capacity as Latin Americans, we are in possession of the best stomach in the world, an eclectic, very free stomach, able to digest, and to digest well, a northern herring or oriental couscous as much as a godwit cooked on an open flame or one of those epic Spanish chorizos.

OLIVERIO

OPEN LETTER
TO *LA PÚA*

Buenos Aires, 31 agosto de 1925.

Señor don Evar Méndez.

Querido Evar: Un libro—y sobre todo un libro de poemas—debe justificarse por sí mismo, sin prólogos que lo defiendan o lo expliquen.

Tú insistes, sin embargo, en la necesidad de que lleve uno la presente edición.

Eludo y condesciendo a tu pedido, adjuntándote la carta que envié a "La Púa", desde París; carta cuyo ingenuo escepticismo podrá, actualmente, hacernos sonreír, pero que tiene, al menos, la ventaja de haber sido escrita contemporáneamente a la publicación de mis 20 poemas.

Te abraza

O. G.

✦

¡Qué quieren ustedes! . . . A veces los nervios se destemplan . . . Se pierde el coraje de continuar sin hacer nada . . . ¡Cansancio de nunca estar cansado! Y se encuentran ritmos al bajar la escalera, poemas tirados en medio de la calle, poemas que uno recoge como quien junta puchos en la vereda.

Lo que sucede entonces es siniestro. El pasatiempo se transforma en oficio. Sentimos pudores de preñez. Nos ruborizamos si alguien nos mira la cabeza. Y lo que es más terrible aún, sin que nos demos cuenta, el oficio termina por interesarnos y es inútil que nos digamos:

OPEN LETTER
TO *LA PÚA*

Buenos Aires, August 31, 1925

Don Evar Méndez

Dear Evar: A book—and above all a book of poems—must justify itself, without prologues to defend or explain it.

You insist, however, on the necessity of the present edition including one.

I will both avoid and consent to your request by enclosing the letter I sent to La Púa from Paris; a letter whose naive skepticism might, nowadays, make us smile, but which at least has the advantage of being written contemporaneously to the publication of my twenty poems.

Warmly

O.G.

✦

What do you want! . . . Sometimes your nerves get frayed . . . You lose the courage to go on without doing anything . . . You tire of never being tired! And when you go down the stairs you find rhythms, poems tossed in the middle of the street, poems that you pick up like someone collecting cigarette butts along the sidewalk.

What happens next is sinister. A hobby becomes a profession. We feel the modesty of pregnancy. We blush if anyone looks us in the face. And what is even more horrible, before we realize it, the profession ends up interesting us and it is useless to tell ourselves "I

7

"Yo no quiero optar, porque optar es osificarse. Yo no quiero tener una actitud, porque todas las actitudes son estúpidas . . . hasta aquella de no tener ninguna . . ."

Irremediablemente terminamos por escribir: *Veinte poemas para ser leídos en el tranvía.*

¿Voluptuosidad de humillarnos ante nuestros propios ojos? ¿Encariñamiento con lo que despreciamos? No lo sé. El hecho es que en lugar de decidir su cremación, condescendemos en enterrar el manuscrito en un cajón de nuestro escritorio, hasta que un buen día, cuando menos podíamos preverlo, comienzan a salir interrogantes por el ojo de la cerradura.

¿Un éxito eventual sería capaz de convencernos de nuestra mediocridad? ¿No tendremos una dosis suficiente de estupidez, como para ser admirados? . . . Hasta que uno contesta a la insinuación de algún amigo: "¿Para qué publicar? Ustedes no lo necesitan para estimarme, los demás . . .", pero como el amigo resulta ser apocalíptico e inexorable, nos replica: "Porque es necesario declararle como tú le has declarado la guerra a la levita, que en nuestro país lleva a todas partes; a la levita con que se escribe en España, cuando no se escribe de golilla, de sotana o en mangas de camisa. Porque es imprescindible tener fe, como tú tienes fe, en nuestra fonética, desde que fuimos nosotros, los americanos, quienes hemos oxigenado el castellano, haciéndolo un idioma respirable, un idioma que puede usarse cotidianamente y escribirse de 'americana', con la 'americana' nuestra de todos los días . . ." Y yo me ruborizo un poco al pensar que acaso tenga fe en nuestra fonética y que nuestra fonética acaso sea tan mal educada como para tener siempre razón . . . y me quedo pensando en nuestra patria, que tiene la imparcialidad de un cuarto de hotel, y me ruborizo un poco al constatar lo difícil que es apegarse a los cuartos de hotel.

¿Publicar? ¿Publicar cuando hasta los mejores publican 1,071% veces más de lo que debieran publicar? . . . Yo no tengo, ni deseo tener,

don't want to choose, to choose is to ossify. I don't want to adopt an attitude because all attitudes are stupid . . . even the attitude of not having an attitude . . ."

Inevitably, we end up writing *Twenty Poems to Be Read on the Streetcar*.

Is it the voluptuousness of humiliating ourselves before our own eyes? Growing fond of the very thing we despise? I don't know. The fact is that rather than choosing cremation, we consent to bury the manuscript in a desk drawer, until one fine day, when we least expect it, question marks begin to emerge from the keyhole.

Will an occasional success convince us of our mediocrity? Won't we have a sufficient dose of stupidity so as to be admired? . . . Until one responds to a friend's insinuations: "Why publish? You don't need it in order to respect me, and as for other people . . ." but as our friend ends up being apocalyptic and inexorable, he answers us: "Because it's necessary to declare it, just as you have declared war on frock coats, which in our country are worn everywhere; the frock coat in which one writes in Spain, when one doesn't write in a ruff collar, cassock, or in shirtsleeves. Because it is essential to have faith, as you have faith, in our phonetics, since it was us, the Americans, who oxygenated Castilian Spanish, making it a breathable language, a language one can use in daily life and write about 'American' things, in our everyday 'American' . . ." And I blush a bit at the thought that perhaps I have faith in our phonetics and that our phonetics perhaps are so rude as to always be right . . . and I'm left thinking about our homeland which has the impartiality of a hotel room, and I blush a little as I recognize how difficult it is to become attached to hotel rooms.

Publish? Publish when even the best publish 1,071% times more than what they ought to publish? . . . I do not have, nor do I wish to have, the blood of a statue. I do not hope to suffer the humiliation of the sparrows. I do not aspire for people to drool all over my grave with

sangre de estatua. Yo no pretendo sufrir la humillación de los gorriones. Yo no aspiro a que me babeen la tumba de lugares comunes, ya que lo único realmente interesante es el mecanismo de sentir y de pensar. ¡Prueba de existencia!

Lo cotidiano, sin embargo, ¿no es una manifestación admirable y modesta de lo absurdo? Y cortar las amarras lógicas, ¿no implica la única y verdadera posibilidad de aventura? ¿Por qué no ser pueriles, ya que sentimos el cansancio de repetir los gestos de los que hace 70 siglos están bajo la tierra? Y ¿cuál sería la razón de no admitir cualquier probabilidad de rejuvenecimiento? ¿No podríamos atribuirle, por ejemplo, todas las responsabilidades a un fetiche perfecto y omnisciente, y tener fe en la plegaria o en la blasfemia, en el albur de un aburrimiento paradisíaco o en la voluptuosidad de condenarnos? ¿Qué nos impediría usar de las virtudes y de los vicios como si fueran ropa limpia, convenir en que el amor no es un narcótico para el uso exclusivo de los imbéciles y ser capaces de pasar junto a la felicidad haciéndonos los distraídos?

Yo, al menos, en mi simpatía por lo contradictorio—sinónimo de vida—no renuncio ni a mi derecho de renunciar, y tiro mis *Veinte poemas*, como una piedra, sonriendo ante la inutilidad de mi gesto.

OLIVERIO GIRONDO
París, diciembre, 1922.

platitudes, since the only truly interesting thing is the mechanism of feeling and thinking. Proof of existence!

But isn't the quotidian an admirable and modest manifestation of the absurd? And to cast off logic's moorings, doesn't that imply the only true possibility for adventure? Why not be puerile, since we are tired of repeating the gestures of those below ground for 70 centuries? And why not admit some probability of rejuvenation? Could we not attribute, for instance, all responsibility to a perfect, omniscient fetish, and have faith in prayer or in blasphemy, in a fate of paradisiacal boredom or in the voluptuousness of self-condemnation? What would stop us from putting on virtues and vices as though they were clean clothes, agreeing that love is not a narcotic for the exclusive use of imbeciles, and being able to get closer to happiness by acting as if we were absent-minded?

I, at least, in my sympathy for the contradictory—a synonym for life—do not even renounce my right to renounce, and I cast my *Twenty Poems* like a stone, smiling at the futility of my gesture.

OLIVERIO GIRONDO
*Paris, December 1922**

---

* Open Letter to *La Púa* was published in 1925 in *Twenty Poems to Be Read on the Streetcar*, Tramway Edition (Edición Tranviaria), but not in the *Twenty Poems to Be Read on the Streetcar* of December 15, 1922. A variant version was also published in *Martín Fierro: A Fortnightly Periodical of Art and Criticism* (March 20, 1924).

PAISAJE BRETÓN

Douarnenez,
en un golpe de cubilete,
empantana
entre sus casas como dados,
un pedazo de mar,
con un olor a sexo que desmaya.

¡Barcas heridas, en seco, con las alas plegadas!
¡Tabernas que cantan con una voz de orangután!

Sobre los muelles,
mercurizados por la pesca,
marineros que se agarran de los brazos

BRETON LANDSCAPE

Douarnenez,
in a throw of the dice cup,
swamps
between its dice-like houses,
a piece of sea
with the fading scent of sex.

Wounded boats, dry-docked, wings folded!
Taverns that sing in an orangutan's voice!

On the docks,
mercurized by fishing,
sailors clasp each other's arms

para aprender a caminar,
y van a estrellarse
con un envión de ola
en las paredes;
mujeres salobres,
enyodadas,
de ojos acuáticos, de cabelleras de alga,
que repasan las redes colgadas de los techos
como velos nupciales.

El campanario de la iglesia,
es un escamoteo de prestidigitación,
saca de su campana
una bandada de palomas.

Mientras las viejecitas,
con sus gorritos de dormir,
entran a la nave
para emborracharse de oraciones,
y para que el silencio
deje de roer por un instante
las narices de piedra de los santos.

Douarnenez, julio 1920.

to learn to walk,
and go crashing
upon a wall
with a wave's jolt;
briny women,
iodized,
with aquatic eyes, seaweed coiffures,
who mend nets hung from the ceiling
like wedding veils.

In a sleight of hand,
the church belfry
pulls from its bell
a flock of doves.

Meanwhile the old women
with their nightcaps
board the nave
to get drunk on prayers;
and so that the silence,
for an instant, will stop gnawing
the stone noses of the saints.

Douarnenez, July 1920

CAFÉ-CONCIERTO

Las notas del pistón describen trayectorias de cohete, vacilan en el aire, se apagan antes de darse contra el suelo.

Salen unos ojos pantanosos, con mal olor, unos dientes podridos por el dulzor de las romanzas, unas piernas que hacen humear el escenario.

La mirada del público tiene más densidad y más calorías que cualquier otra, es una mirada corrosiva que atraviesa las mallas y apergamina la piel de las artistas.

Hay un grupo de marineros encandilados ante el faro que un "maquereau" tiene en el dedo meñique, una reunión de prostitutas con un relente a puerto, un inglés que fabrica niebla con sus pupilas y su pipa.

La camarera me trae, en una bandeja lunar, sus senos semidesnudos . . . unos senos que me llevaría para calentarme los pies cuando me acueste.

El telón, al cerrarse, simula un telón entreabierto.

Brest, agosto 1920.

CAFÉ-CONCERT

The piston's notes trace rocket trajectories, waver in air, extinguish before they hit the ground.

Out come swampy eyes with a foul odor, teeth rotten from dulcet airs, legs steaming up the stage.

This audience's gaze has more density, more calories, than any other; it's a corrosive gaze that penetrates the tights and parches the artists' skin.

There's a group of sailors, dazzled by the beacon a *maquereau* wears on his pinky; the whores have an appointment with the chill in the port; an Englishman fabricates fog with his pupils and pipe.

The waitress brings me, on a lunar tray, her semi-bared breasts . . . breasts I will take to warm my feet when I retire to bed.

The curtain, on closing, simulates a half-open curtain.

Brest, August 1920

17

CROQUIS EN LA ARENA

La mañana se pasea en la playa empolvada de sol.

Brazos.
Piernas amputadas.
Cuerpos que se reintegran.
Cabezas flotantes de caucho.

Al tornearles los cuerpos a las bañistas,
las olas alargan sus virutas sobre el
aserrín de la playa.

¡Todo es oro y azul!

La sombra de los toldos.
Los ojos de las chicas que se inyectan
novelas y horizontes. Mi alegría,
de zapatos de goma, que me hace
rebotar sobre la arena.

SKETCH IN THE SAND

Morning wanders the beach, powdered with sun.

Arms.
Amputated legs.
Bodies that reassemble themselves.
Rubber floating heads.

Turning the bathers' bodies like a lathe,
the waves stretch shavings over the
beach's sawdust.

All is gold and blue!

The canopies' shadow.
The eyes of girls who inject them-
selves with novels and horizons. My
rubber-soled happiness makes me
bounce over the sand.

Por ochenta centavos, los fotógrafos venden los cuerpos de las mujeres que se bañan.

Hay kioscos que explotan la dramaticidad de la rompiente. Sirvientas cluecas. Sifones irascibles, con extracto de mar. Rocas con pechos algosos de marinero y corazones pintados de esgrimista. Bandadas de gaviotas, que fingen el vuelo destrozado de un pedazo blanco de papel.

¡Y ante todo está el mar!

¡El mar! . . . ritmo de divagaciones. ¡El mar! con su baba y con su epilepsia.

¡El mar! . . . hasta gritar

¡BASTA!

como en el circo.

Mar del Plata, octubre 1920.

For eighty *centavos* the photographers sell the bodies of bathing women.

There are newsstands exploiting the drama of the breakers. Broody maids. Irascible sodas with extract of sea. Rocks with a sailor's algal breast and a fencer's painted heart. Flocks of seagulls feign the broken flight of a sheet of white paper.

And in the foreground is the sea!

The sea! . . . rhythm of digressions. The sea! with its drool and its epilepsy.

The sea! . . . until you shout

ENOUGH!

as you do at the circus.

Mar del Plata, October 1920

NOCTURNO

Frescor de los vidrios al apoyar la frente en la ventana. Luces trasnochadas que al apagarse nos dejan todavía más solos. Telaraña que los alambres tejen sobre las azoteas. Trote hueco de los jamelgos que pasan y nos emocionan sin razón.

¿A qué nos hace recordar el aullido de los gatos en celo, y cuál será la intención de los papeles que se arrastran en los patios vacíos?

Hora en que los muebles viejos aprovechan para sacarse las mentiras, y en que las cañerías tienen gritos estrangulados, como si se asfixiaran dentro de las paredes.

A veces se piensa, al dar vuelta la llave de la electricidad, en el espanto que sentirán las sombras, y quisiéramos avisarles para que tuvieran tiempo de acurrucarse en los rincones. Y a veces las cruces de los postes telefónicos, sobre las azoteas, tienen algo de siniestro y uno quisiera rozarse a las paredes, como un gato o como un ladrón.

Noches en las que desearíamos que nos pasaran la mano por el lomo, y en las que súbitamente se comprende que no hay ternura comparable a la de acariciar algo que duerme.

¡Silencio!—grillo afónico que se nos mete en el oído—. ¡Cantar de las canillas mal cerradas!—único grillo que le conviene a la ciudad—

Buenos Aires, noviembre 1921.

NOCTURNE

Cool glass, when leaning forehead against window. Late-night lights go out, leaving us even lonelier. Spider webs woven by wires over rooftops. For no reason, the hollow trot of passing nags makes us emotional.

What does the howl of these cats in heat call to mind, and what can the scraps of paper be plotting as they slither onto empty patios?

The time of night when old furniture seizes the chance to shed its lies, when pipes make strangulated cries, as though suffocating inside the walls.

Now and then we think, when flipping the electric light switch, of the fright the shadows must feel, and we'd like to warn them so they have time to curl up in the corners. And now and then there is something sinister about the telephone-pole crosses over the rooftops, and one wants to slink along the walls like a cat or a thief.

Nights when we wish for a hand to caress our lower back, when we suddenly realize that no tenderness compares to stroking something as it sleeps.

Silence!—voiceless cricket that hops in our ear. Leaky faucet song!— the only cricket that suits the city.

Buenos Aires, November 1921

RIO DE JANEIRO

La ciudad imita en cartón, una ciudad de pórfido.

Caravanas de montañas acampan en los alrededores.

El "Pan de Azúcar" basta para almibarar toda la bahía . . .
El "Pan de Azúcar" y su alambre carril, que perderá el equilibrio
por no usar una sombrilla de papel.

Con sus caras pintarrajeadas, los edificios saltan unos encima de
otros y cuando están arriba, ponen el lomo, para que las palmeras les
den un golpe de plumero en la azotea.

RIO DE JANEIRO

The city is a cardboard imitation of a porphyry city.

Caravans of mountains encamp in the outskirts.

Sugarloaf Mountain is enough to bathe the whole bay in syrup . . .
Sugarloaf Mountain and its cable car that will lose its balance
because it doesn't carry a paper parasol.

With their garishly painted faces, the buildings leap over one
another, and once they reach the top, they stick out their backsides
so the palm trees can give their roof a whack with a feather duster.

El sol ablanda el asfalto y las nalgas de las mujeres, madura las peras de la electricidad, sufre un crepúsculo, en los botones de ópalo que los hombres usan hasta para abrocharse la braqueta.

¡Siete veces al día, se riegan las calles con agua de jazmín!

Hay viejos árboles pederastas, florecidos en rosas té; y viejos árboles que se tragan los chicos que juegan al arco en los paseos. Frutas que al caer hacen un huraco enorme en la vereda; negros que tienen cutis de tabaco, las palmas de las manos hechas de coral, y sonrisas desfachatadas de sandía.

Sólo por cuatrocientos mil reis se toma un café, que perfuma todo un barrio de la ciudad durante diez minutos.

Río de Janeiro, noviembre 1920.

The sun softens asphalt and ladies' buttocks, ripens pears of electricity, endures a dusk in the opal buttons men use even to fasten their flies.

Seven times a day the streets are hosed down with jasmine water!

There are old pederast trees blossoming in tea rose; and old trees that swallow the kids playing goalie in the walkways. Fruits make enormous hollows in the sidewalk when they fall; tobacco-complexioned blacks, palms made of coral, brazen smiles of watermelons.

For only four hundred thousand *reis*, you can drink a cup of coffee that will perfume a whole city neighborhood for ten minutes.

Río de Janeiro, November 1920

APUNTE CALLEJERO

En la terraza de un café hay una familia gris. Pasan unos senos bizcos buscando una sonrisa sobre las mesas. El ruido de los automóviles destiñe las hojas de los árboles. En un quinto piso, alguien se crucifica al abrir de par en par una ventana.

Pienso en dónde guardaré los kioscos, los faroles, los transeúntes, que se me entran por las pupilas. Me siento tan lleno que tengo miedo de estallar . . . Necesitaría dejar algún lastre sobre la vereda . . .

Al llegar a una esquina, mi sombra se separa de mí, y de pronto, se arroja entre las ruedas de un tranvía.

STREET NOTE

A gray family sits on the café terrace. Cross-eyed breasts pass by, surveying the tables for a smile. The sound of motorcars blanches the tree leaves. On the fifth floor someone is crucified, throwing the window wide open.

I think about where I will store the kiosks, streetlamps, passersby that enter through my pupils. I feel so full I fear I'll burst . . . I might need to drop some ballast on the walkway . . .

When I arrive at a corner, my shadow separates from me and suddenly throws itself under the wheels of a streetcar.

MILONGA

Sobre las mesas, botellas decapitadas de "champagne" con corbatas blancas de payaso, baldes de níquel que trasuntan enflaquecidos brazos y espaldas de "cocottes".

El bandoneón canta con esperezos de gusano baboso, contradice el pelo rojo de la alfombra, imanta los pezones, los pubis y la punta de los zapatos.

MILONGA

On the tables, decapitated bottles of *champagne* with clownish white neckties, nickel pails whose reflection slims the *cocottes'* arms and back.

The *bandoneón* sings with the lazy stretch of a lovestruck worm, conflicts with the carpet's red hair, magnetizes nipples, pubises, and shoe tips.

Machos que se quiebran en un corte ritual, la cabeza hundida entre los hombros, la jeta hinchada de palabras soeces.

Hembras con las ancas nerviosas, un poquitito de espuma en las axilas, y los ojos demasiado aceitados.

De pronto se oye un fracaso de cristales. Las mesas dan un corcovo y pegan cuatro patadas en el aire. Un enorme espejo se derrumba con las columnas y la gente que tenía dentro; mientras entre un oleaje de brazos y de espaldas estallan las trompadas, como una rueda de cohetes de bengala.

Junto con el vigilante, entra la aurora vestida de violeta.

Buenos Aires, octubre 1921.

Males who bend in half with a ritual slice, head sunk between their shoulders, mugs inflated with crude words.

Females with fidgety haunches, a little foam in their armpits and over-oiled eyes.

Suddenly you hear glass breaking. The tables buck and give four kicks in the air. An enormous mirror collapses along with the columns and the people inside; while in a tide of arms and backs, punches flare like a burst of Bengal lights.

Together with the watchman, dawn enters dressed in violet.

Buenos Aires, October 1921

VENECIA

Se respira una brisa de tarjeta postal.

¡Terrazas! Góndolas con ritmos de cadera. Fachadas que reintegran tapices persas en el agua. Remos que no terminan nunca de llorar.

El silencio hace gárgaras en los umbrales, arpegia un "pizzicato" en las amarras, roe el misterio de las casas cerradas.

Al pasar debajo de los puentes, uno aprovecha para ponerse colorado.

Bogan en la Laguna, "dandys" que usan un lacrimatorio en el bolsillo con todas las iridiscencias del canal, mujeres que han traído sus labios de Viena y de Berlín para saborear una carne de color aceituna, y mujeres que sólo se alimentan de pétalos de rosa, tienen las manos incrustadas de ojos de serpiente, y la quijada fatal de las heroínas d'Annunzianas.

¡Cuando el sol incendia la ciudad, es obligatorio ponerse un alma de Nerón!

En los "piccoli canali" los gondoleros fornican con la noche, anunciando su espasmo con un triste cantar, mientras la luna engorda, como en cualquier parte, su mofletudo visaje de portera.

VENICE

A postcard breeze blows.

Terraces! Gondolas with the rhythm of hips. Façades weaving Persian rugs back into the water. Oars that never stop sobbing.

Silence gurgles in the thresholds, plucks a *pizzicato* among the moorings, gnaws at the mystery of shuttered houses.

Passing under the bridges, you take advantage of the chance to blush.

Rowing in the Lagoon are *dandies* who keep in their pockets a lachrymatory with all the canal's iridescences, women who have brought their lips from Vienna and Berlin to taste olive-colored flesh, and women nourished only by rose petals, hands encrusted with serpent eyes, the fatal jaws of d'Annunzian heroines.

When the sun torches the city, all must don a soul like Nero's!

In the *piccoli canali* the gondoliers fornicate with the night, announcing their spasm with a sad song, while the moon's chubby-cheeked porter face, just like everywhere, grows fat.

Yo dudo que aún en esta ciudad de sensualismo, existan falos más llamativos, y de una erección más precipitada, que la de los badajos del "campanile" de San Marcos.

Venecia, julio 1921.

I doubt that even in this city of sensualism, there are more eye-catching phalluses, with hastier erections, than the clappers on Saint Mark's *campanile.*

Venice, July 1921

EXVOTO

A las chicas de Flores

Las chicas de Flores, tienen los ojos dulces, como las almendras azucaradas de la Confitería del Molino, y usan moños de seda que les liban las nalgas en un aleteo de mariposa.

Las chicas de Flores, se pasean tomadas de los brazos, para transmitirse sus estremecimientos, y si alguien las mira en las pupilas, aprietan las piernas, de miedo de que el sexo se les caiga en la vereda.

Al atardecer, todas ellas cuelgan sus pechos sin madurar del ramaje de hierro de los balcones, para que sus vestidos se empurpuren al sentirlas desnudas, y de noche, a remolque de sus mamás—empavesadas como fragatas—van a pasearse por la plaza, para que los hombres les

EX-VOTO

To the Girls of Flores

The Flores girls have sweet eyes, like the candied almonds at the Confitería El Molino, and they wear silk ribbons that sip at their buttocks with the flutter of a butterfly.

The Flores girls go arm-in-arm, transmitting their tremors to one another, and if anyone looks them in the pupils, their legs squeeze shut out of fear that their sex will fall on the sidewalk.

At dusk, all of them hang their unripe breasts from the iron branchwork of the balconies, so that their dresses blush purple when they feel their nakedness, and at night, towed by their mothers—decked out with bunting like frigates—they go for a stroll in the plaza so that men can

eyaculen palabras al oído, y sus pezones fosforescentes se enciendan y se apaguen como luciérnagas.

Las chicas de Flores, viven en la angustia de que las nalgas se les pudran, como manzanas que se han dejado pasar, y el deseo de los hombres las sofoca tanto, que a veces quisieran desembarazarse de él como de un corsé, ya que no tienen el coraje de cortarse el cuerpo a pedacitos y arrojárselo, a todos los que les pasan la vereda.

Buenos Aires, octubre 1920.

ejaculate words in their ears, and their phosphorescent nipples turn on and off like fireflies.

The Flores girls live with the anxiety that their buttocks will go bad, like apples allowed to overripen, and men's desire suffocates them so much that sometimes they want to shed it like a corset, since they lack the courage to cut their bodies into pieces and toss them to everyone who passes them on the sidewalk.

Buenos Aires, October 1920

FIESTA EN DAKAR

La calle pasa con olor a desierto, entre un friso de negros sentados sobre el cordón de la vereda.

Frente al Palacio de la Gobernación:

¡CALOR! ¡CALOR!

Europeos que usan una escupidera en la cabeza. Negros estilizados con ademanes de sultán.

El candombe les bate las ubres a las mujeres para que al pasar, el ministro les ordeñe una taza de chocolate.

¡Plantas callicidas! Negras vestidas de papagayo, con sus crías en uno de los pliegues de la falda. Palmeras, que de noche se estiran para sacarle a las estrellas el polvo que se les ha entrado en la pupila.

¡Habrá cohetes! ¡Cañonazos! Un nuevo impuesto a los nativos. Discursos en cuatro mil lenguas oscuras.

Y de noche:

¡ILUMINACIÓN!

a cargo de las constelaciones.

HOLIDAY IN DAKAR

The street goes by smelling of desert, amid a frieze of blacks sitting on the curb.

In front of the Palace of the Interior:

HEAT! HEAT!

Europeans who wear spittoons on their heads. Slender black men with a sultan's gestures.

The *candombé* makes women's udders churn so that the minister, when he goes by, milks hot chocolate from them.

Corn-cured soles! Black women dressed as parrots, with their young in their skirt folds. Palm trees that, at night, reach up to brush away the dust that's gotten in the stars' eyes.

There will be fireworks! Cannon shots! A new tax on the natives. Conversations in four thousand obscure tongues.

And at night:

ILLUMINATION!

courtesy of the constellations.

43

CROQUIS SEVILLANO

El sol pone una ojera violácea en el alero de las casas, apergamina la epidermis de las camisas ahorcadas en medio de la calle.

¡Ventanas con aliento y labios de mujer!

Pasan perros con caderas de bailarín. Chulos con los pantalones lustrados al betún. Jamelgos que el domingo se arrancarán las tripas en la plaza de toros.

SEVILLIAN SKETCH

The sun paints violet bags under the eyes of the eaves, parches the epidermis of shirts hung in the middle of the street.

Windows with a woman's lips and breath!

Dogs go by with dancer's hips. Pimps whose pants have a shoe-polish shine. Nags that will have their intestines ripped out in the Plaza de Toros on Sunday.

¡Los patios fabrican azahares y noviazgos!

Hay una capa prendida a una reja con crispaciones de murciélago. Un cura de Zurbarán, que vende a un anticuario una casulla robada en la sacristía. Unos ojos excesivos, que sacan llagas al mirar.

Las mujeres tienen los poros abiertos como ventositas y una temperatura siete décimos más elevada que la normal.

Sevilla, marzo 1920.

The patios manufacture lemon blossoms and courtships!

There is a cape caught on a railing with the agitations of a bat. A Zurbarán priest sells an antique dealer a chasuble robbed from the sacristy. Excessive eyes cause wounds when they gaze.

The women have pores as open as little cupping glasses and a temperature seven-tenths above normal.

Seville, March 1920

CORSO

La banda de música le chasquea el lomo
para que siga dando vueltas
cloroformado bajo los antifaces
con su olor a pomo y a sudor
y su voz falsa
y sus adioses de naufragio
y su cabellera desgreñada de largas tiras de papel
que los árboles le peinan al pasar
junto al cordón de la vereda
donde las gentes
le tiran pequeños salvavidas de todos los colores
mientras las chicas
se sacan los senos de las batas
para arrojárselos a las comparsas
que espiritualizan
en un suspiro de papel de seda
su cansancio de querer ser feliz
que apenas tiene fuerzas para llegar
a la altura de las bombitas de luz eléctrica.

Mar del Plata, febrero 1921.

CARNIVAL PARADE

The band of musicians cracks their backs
to keep spinning
chloroformed beneath the masks
with their pomaceous scent and sweat
and their false voices
and their shipwrecked farewells
and their disheveled hair made of long paper strips
that the trees comb when passing
close to the curb
where people
throw them little life rings of every color
while the girls
lift their breasts from their robes
to fling them to the troupes
who sublimate
in a silk paper sigh
how weary they are of wanting to be happy
and scarcely have the strength to rise
as high as the electric light bulbs.

Mar del Plata, February 1921

BIARRITZ

El casino sorbe las últimas gotas de crepúsculo.

Automóviles afónicos. Escaparates constelados de estrellas falsas. Mujeres que van a perder sus sonrisas al bacará.

Con la cara desteñida por el tapete, los "croupiers" ofician, los ojos bizcos de tanto ver pasar dinero.

¡Pupilas que se licuan al dar vuelta las cartas!
¡Collares de perlas que hunden un tarascón en las gargantas!

BIARRITZ

The casino sips the last drops of dusk.

Hoarse automobiles. Shop windows constellated with fake stars. Women who will lose their smiles playing baccarat.

Faces discolored by the felt, the *croupiers* officiate, cross-eyed from so much money watching.

Pupils liquefy when the cards are flipped over!
Pearl necklaces sink their teeth into throats!

Hay efebos barbilampiños que usan una bragueta en el trasero. Hombres con baberos de porcelana. Un señor con un cuello que terminará por estrangularlo. Unas tetas que saltarán de un momento a otro de un escote, y lo arrollarán todo, como dos enormes bolas de billar.

Cuando la puerta se entreabre, entra un pedazo de "Fox-trot".

Biarritz, octubre 1920.

There are lightly bearded ephebes with their flies in the rear. Men with porcelain bibs. A gentleman with a collar that will end up strangling him. Tits that could jump from a neckline at any moment and roll over everything like two huge billiard balls.

When the door half-opens, in comes a bit of *fox-trot*.

Biarritz, October 1920

OTRO NOCTURNO

La luna, como la esfera luminosa del reloj de un edificio público.

¡Faroles enfermos de ictericia! ¡Faroles con gorras de "apache", que fuman un cigarrillo en las esquinas!

¡Canto humilde y humillado de los mingitorios cansados de cantar! ¡Y silencio de las estrellas, sobre el asfalto humedecido!

¿Por qué, a veces, sentiremos una tristeza parecida a la de un par de medias tirado en un rincón? y ¿por qué, a veces, nos interesará tanto el partido de pelota que el eco de nuestros pasos juega en la pared?

Noches en las que nos disimulamos bajo la sombra de los árboles, de miedo de que las casas se despierten de pronto y nos vean pasar, ¡y en las que el único consuelo es la seguridad de que nuestra cama nos espera, con las velas tendidas hacia un país mejor!

París, julio 1921.

ANOTHER NOCTURNE

The moon, like a clock's luminous sphere on a public building.

Streetlamps sick with jaundice! Streetlamps in *Apache* caps, smoking cigarettes on the corners!

Humble and humiliated song of urinals tired of singing! And the stars' silence above the damp asphalt.

Why, sometimes, do we feel sadness like a pair of stockings tossed in a corner? And why, sometimes, do we become so interested in the ballgame our echoing footsteps play against the wall?

Nights when we hide in the shadows of the trees, afraid the houses will suddenly wake up and see us passing by, when our sole consolation is the certainty that our bed awaits us, with candles lighting the way to a better country.

Paris, July 1921

PEDESTRE

En el fondo de la calle, un edificio público aspira el mal olor de la ciudad.

Las sombras se quiebran el espinazo en los umbrales, se acuestan para fornicar en la vereda.

Con un brazo prendido a la pared, un farol apagado tiene la visión convexa de la gente que pasa en automóvil.

Las miradas de los transeúntes ensucian las cosas que se exhiben en los escaparates, adelgazan las piernas que cuelgan bajo las capotas de las victorias.

Junto al cordón de la vereda un kiosco acaba de tragarse una mujer.

PEDESTRIAN

At the end of the street, a public building inhales the city's stink.

Shadows break their backs on the threshold, lie down to fornicate on the sidewalk.

One arm fastened to the wall, an extinguished streetlamp takes a convex view of people who pass in motorcars.

The gaze of passersby dirties the shop window displays, slims down the legs that dangle beneath the Victorias' hoods.

By the curb, a kiosk just swallowed a woman.

Pasa: una inglesa idéntica a un farol. Un tranvía que es un colegio sobre ruedas. Un perro fracasado, con ojos de prostituta que nos da vergüenza mirarlo y dejarlo pasar.*

De repente: el vigilante de la esquina detiene de un golpe de batuta todos los estremecimientos de la ciudad, para que se oiga en un solo susurro, el susurro de todos los senos al rozarse.

Buenos Aires, agosto 1920.

---

* Los perros fracasados han perdido a su dueño por levantar la pata como una mandolina, el pellejo les ha quedado demasiado grande, tienen una voz afónica de alcoholista y son capaces de estirarse en un umbral, para que los barran junto con la basura.

Passing by: an Englishwoman identical to a streetlamp. A streetcar that's a school on wheels. A ruined dog with a prostitute's eyes who shames us when we look at him and let him go by.*

Suddenly: with a stroke of his baton, the corner watchman halts every shiver in the city, so that you can hear in a single whisper, the whisper of all breasts brushing against one another.

Buenos Aires, August 1920

---

* Ruined dogs have lost their owners by raising a paw like a mandolin, their hides are too big for them, they have the hoarse voice of an alcoholist, and they are known to stretch out in the doorway to be swept up with the trash.

CHIOGGIA

Entre un bosque de mástiles,
y con sus muelles empavesados de camisas,
Chioggia
fondea en la laguna,
ensangrentada de crepúsculo
y de velas latinas.

¡Redes tendidas sobre calles musgosas . . . sin afeitar!
¡Aire que nos calafatea los pulmones, dejándonos un gusto de alquitrán!

Mientras las mujeres
se gastan las pupilas
tejiendo puntillas de neblina,
desde el lomo de los puentes,
los chicos se zambullen
en la basura del canal.

¡Marineros con cutis de pasa de higo y como garfios los dedos de los pies!
Marineros que remiendan las velas en los umbrales y se ciñen con ella
la cintura, como con una falda suntuosa y con olor a mar.

Al atardecer, un olor a frituras agranda los estómagos,
mientras los zuecos comienzan a cantar . . .

CHIOGGIA

Amid a forest of masts,
and with its shirt-bedecked quays,
Chioggia
anchors in the lagoon,
bloodstained by dusk
and lateen sails.

Nets hung out over mossy streets . . . unshaven!
Air that caulks our lungs, leaving us with the taste of tar!

While the women
wear out their pupils
weaving lace-edges of mist,
from the backs of the bridges,
the boys dunk each other
in the trash of the canal.

Sailors with wrinkled fig skin and toes like hooks!
Sailors mending sails in the doorways and belting their waists with
them like sumptuous skirts scented with sea.

At dusk, the smell of frying expands stomachs,
while wooden clogs begin to sing . . .

Y de noche, la luna, al disgregarse en el canal, finge un enjambre de peces plateados alrededor de una carnaza.

Venecia, julio 1921.

And at night, as the moon disintegrates in the canal, it pretends to be a school of silver fish swarming around bait.

Venice, July 1921

PLAZA

Los árboles filtran un ruido de ciudad.

Caminos que se enrojecen al abrazar la rechonchez de los parterres. Idilios que explican cualquiera negligencia culinaria. Hombres anestesiados de sol, que no se sabe si se han muerto.

La vida aquí es urbana y es simple.

Sólo la complican:

Uno de esos hombres con bigotes de muñeco de cera, que enloquecen a las amas de cría y les ordeñan todo lo que han ganado con sus ubres.

PLAZA

The trees filter the city sound.

Paths that blush when they embrace the plumpness of the flower beds. Love affairs explain away all culinary negligence. Men so anesthetized by sun you don't know if they're dead.

Life here is urban, and simple.

The only complications:

One of those men with a wax-doll mustache, who drives the wet nurses crazy and milks them for all their udder-gotten gains.

El guardián con su bomba, que es un "Manneken-Pis".

Una señora que hace gestos de semáforo a un vigilante, al sentir que sus mellizos se están estrangulando en su barriga.

Buenos Aires, diciembre 1920.

The guard with his paunch is a *Manneken-Pis.*

A woman makes traffic signals to a watchman when she feels her twins strangling each other in her belly.

Buenos Aires, December 1920

LAGO MAYOR

Al pedir el boleto hay que "impostar" la voz.

¡ISOLA BELLA! ¡ISOLA BELLA!

Isola Bella, tiene justo el grandor que queda bien, en la tela que pintan las inglesas.

Isola Bella, con su palacio y hasta con el lema del escudo de sus puertas de pórfido:

"HUMILITAS"

¡Salones! Salones de artesonados tormentosos donde cuatrocientas cariátides se hacen cortes de manga entre una bandada de angelitos.

"HUMILITAS"

Alcobas con lechos de topacio que exigen que quien se acueste en ellos se ponga por lo menos una "aigrette" de ave de paraíso en el trasero.

"HUMILITAS"

Jardines que se derraman en el lago en una cascada de terrazas, y donde los pavos reales abren sus blancas sombrillas de encaje, para

LAKE MAGGIORE

To ask for a ticket you have to "project" your voice.

ISOLA BELLA! ISOLA BELLA!

Isola Bella is just the right size on the canvases the English ladies paint.

Isola Bella, with its palace and even with a motto from the crest on its porphyry gates:

"HUMILITAS"

Salons! Salons with stormily coffered ceilings, where four hundred caryatids give an up-yours amid a flock of little angels.

"HUMILITAS"

Bedrooms with topaz beds requiring whoever lies in them to pin at least a bird-of-paradise aigrette to their backside.

"HUMILITAS"

Gardens that spill into the lake in a cascade of terraces, and where the peacocks open their white lace parasols to shield themselves from

taparse el sol o barren, con sus escobas incrustadas de zafiros y de rubíes, los caminos ensangrentados de amapolas.

"HUMILITAS"

Jardines donde los guardianes lustran las hojas de los árboles para que al pasar, nos arreglemos la corbata, y que—ante la desnudez de las Venus que pueblan los boscajes—nos brindan una rama de alcanfor ...

¡ISOLA BELLA! ...

Isola Bella, sin duda, es el paisaje que queda bien, en la tela que pintan las inglesas.

Isola Bella, con su palacio y hasta con el lema del escudo de sus puertas de pórfido:

"HUMILITAS"

Pallanza, abril 1922.

the sun, or sweep, with their brooms encrusted with sapphires and rubies, the poppy-bloodied paths.

"HUMILITAS"

Gardens where the guards polish the tree leaves so that we straighten our ties when we go by, and—in presence of the nude Venuses peopling the thicket—they offer us a branch of camphor.

ISOLA BELLA! . . .

Isola Bella, no doubt about it, is the landscape that's just right on the canvases the English ladies paint.

Isola Bella, with its palace and with even a motto from the crest on its porphyry gates:

"HUMILITAS"

Pallanza, April 1922

SEVILLANO

En el atrio: una reunión de ciegos auténticos, hasta con placa, una jauría de chicuelos, que ladra por una perra.

La iglesia se refrigera para que no se le derritan los ojos y los brazos . . . de los exvotos.

SEVILLIAN

In the atrium: a meeting of the authentically blind, badges and all;
a gang of kids barking at a bitch.

The church cools down to avoid melting the eyes and arms . . . of
the votives.

Bajo sus mantos rígidos, las vírgenes enjugan lágrimas de rubí. Algunas tienen cabelleras de cola de caballo. Otras usan de alfiletero el corazón.

Un cencerro de llaves impregna la penumbra de un pesado olor a sacristía. Al persignarse revive en una vieja un ancestral orangután.

Y mientras, frente al altar mayor, a las mujeres se les licua el sexo contemplando un crucifijo que sangra por sus sesenta y seis costillas, el cura mastica una plegaria como un pedazo de "chewing gum".

Sevilla, abril 1920.

Beneath their rigid mantles the Virgins wipe away ruby tears. Some wear ponytails. Others use their hearts as pincushions.

A cowbell of keys impregnates the penumbra with the sacristy's heavy stench. As an old woman crosses herself, an ancestral orangutan within her revives.

And at the grand altar, while the ladies' sexes deliquesce contemplating a crucifix bleeding from its sixty-six ribs, the priest chomps a prayer like a stick of "chewing gum."

Seville, April 1920

VERONA

¡Se celebra el adulterio de María con la Paloma Sacra!

Una lluvia pulverizada lustra "La Plaza de las Verduras", se hincha en globitos que navegan por la vereda y de repente estallan sin motivo.

Entre los dedos de las arcadas, una multitud espesa amasa su desilusión; mientras, la banda gruñe un tiempo de vals, para que los estandartes den cuatro vueltas y se paren.

La Virgen, sentada en una fuente, como sobre un "bidé", derrama un agua enrojecida por las bombitas de luz eléctrica que le han puesto en los pies.

¡Guitarras! ¡Mandolinas! ¡Balcones sin escalas y sin Julietas! Paraguas que sudan y son como la supervivencia de una flora ya fósil. Capiteles donde unos monos se entretienen desde hace nueve siglos en hacer el amor.

El cielo simple, verdoso, un poco sucio, es del mismo color que el uniforme de los soldados.

Verona, julio 1921.

VERONA

Celebrate Mary's adultery with the Holy Dove!

Pulverized rain polishes La Plaza de las Verduras, the little balloons that cruise down the sidewalk inflate and suddenly explode for no reason.

Between the fingers of the arcades, a dense crowd kneads its disillusionment; meanwhile, the band grumbles out a waltz beat so the standard bearers turn four times and stop.

The Virgin, seated on a fountain as if on a bidet, spills water reddened by the little electric light bulbs placed on her feet.

Guitars! Mandolins! Balconies lacking ladders or Juliet vines! Umbrellas are sweating like the survival of flora turned fossil. Cornices where some monkeys have been amusing themselves for nine centuries by making love.

Green, a bit dirty, the simple sky is the same color as the soldiers' uniforms.

Verona, July 1921

DECALCOMANIA

CALPE - MADRID - 1925

¡España! . . . país ardiente y seco
como un repiqueteo de castañuelas.
¡España! . . . sugestión cálida y persistente
como un bordoneo de guitarra.

Lo bueno, si breve, dos veces bueno.
Lo malo, si poco, no tan malo.

Gracián

Spain! Ardent and dry
like a click of the castanets.
Spain! Warm, persistent suggestion
like a strum of the guitar.

The good, when brief, is twice as good.
The bad, when scarce, is not so bad.

Gracián

TOLEDO

A D. Enrique Díez-Canedo.

Forjada en la "Fábrica de Armas y Municiones",
la ciudad
muerde con sus almenas
un pedazo de cielo,
mientras el Tajo,
alfanje que se funde en un molde de piedra,
atraviesa los puentes y la Vega,
pintada por algún primitivo castellano
de esos que conservaron
una influencia flamenca.

Ya al subir en dirección a la ciudad,
apriétase en las llaves
la empuñadura de una espada,
en tanto que un vientecillo
nos va enmoheciendo el espinazo
para insuflarnos el empaque
que los aduaneros exigen al entrar.

¡Silencio!
¡Silencio que nos extravía las pupilas
y nos diafaniza la nariz!

TOLEDO

To D. Enrique Díez-Canedo

Forged in the "Factory of Arms and Munitions,"
the city
bites a piece of sky
with its battlements,
while the Tagus,
cutlass melting in a stone cast,
crosses the bridges and the Vega,
painted by one of those primitive Castilians
who preserved
some Flemish influence.

Now as it heads to the city,
among the locks
a sword's hilt is clenched,
even as a little breeze
keeps mildewing our backbone
to pump the filtering mechanism
the customs officers require upon entry.

Silence!
Silence that sets our eyes roaming
and sanitizes our sinuses!

¡Silencio!

Perros que se pasean de golilla
con los ojos pintados por el Greco.
Posadas donde se hospedan todavía
los protagonistas del "Lazarillo" y del "Buscón".
Puertas que gruñen y se cierran
con las llaves que se le extraviaron a San Pedro.

¡Para cruzar sobre las murallas y el Alcázar
las nubes ensillan con arneses y paramentos
medioevales!

Hidalgos que se alimentan de piedras y de orgullo,
tienen la carne idéntica a la cera de los exvotos
y un tufo a herrumbre y a ratón.
Hidalgos que se detienen para escupir
con la jactancia con que sus abuelos
tiraban su escarcela a los leprosos.

Los pies ensangrentados por los guijarros,
se gulusmea en las cocinas
un olorcillo a inquisición,
y cuando las sombras se descuelgan de los tejados,
se oye la gesta
que las paredes nos cuentan al pasar,
a cuyo influjo una pelambre
nos va cubriendo las tetillas.

¡Noches en que los pasos suenan
como malas palabras!
¡Noches, con gélido aliento de fantasma,

84

Silence!

Dogs pass in ruff collars
with eyes painted by el Greco.
Inns that still host
the protagonists from *Lazarillo* and *Buscón*.
Doors that groan and lock
with the keys Saint Peter misplaced.

To cross the city walls and the Alcázar,
the clouds are saddled with harnesses and medieval vestments!

Hidalgos who feed on stones and pride
have flesh identical to ex-voto wax
and the stench of rust and rodents.
Hidalgos who pause to spit
with the hauteur of their grandparents
tossing their purses to lepers.

Feet bloodied by pebbles,
you catch a whiff of Inquisition
from the kitchens,
and when shadows detach from the rooftops,
you can hear the walls
recounting their heroic deeds as we pass,
which makes a tuft of hair
grow on our nipples.

Nights when footsteps
ring like curse words!
Nights with the icy breath of ghosts,

en que las piedras que circundan la población
celebran aquelarres goyescos!

¡Juro,
por el mismísimo Cristo de la Vega,
que a pesar del cansancio que nos purifica
y nos despoja de toda vanidad,
a veces, al atravesar una calleja,
uno se cree Don Juan!

Toledo, abril 1923.

when the stones encircling the town
celebrate in a Goyaesque witches' sabbath.

I swear it,
by the Cristo de la Vega himself,
that despite the sleep that purifies us
and strips us of all vanity,
now and then, crossing a narrow street,
you think you're Don Juan!

Toledo, April 1923

CALLE DE LAS SIERPES

A D. Ramón Gómez de la Serna.

Una corriente de brazos y de espaldas
nos encauza
y nos hace desembocar
bajo los abanicos,
las pipas,
los anteojos enormes
colgados en medio de la calle;
únicos testimonios de una raza
desaparecida de gigantes.

Sentados al borde de las sillas,
cual si fueran a dar un brinco
y ponerse a bailar,
los parroquianos de los cafés
aplauden la actividad del camarero,
mientras los limpiabotas les lustran los zapatos
hasta que pueda leerse
el anuncio de la corrida del domingo.

Con sus caras de mascarón de proa,
el habano hace las veces de bauprés,
los hacendados penetran
en los despachos de bebidas,

LAS SIERPES STREET

To D. Ramón Gómez de la Serna

A current of arms and backs
channels us
and pours us out
under the fans,
the pipes,
the huge eyeglasses
hanging in the middle of the street;
the only evidence of a vanished
race of giants.

At the edge of their seats,
as if ready to leap up
and start dancing,
the café regulars
applaud the waiter's movements,
while the bootblacks polish their shoes
until you can read the ad
for Sunday's bullfight in their shine.

With faces like figureheads,
Cuban cigars serving as bowsprits,
the landowners burst into
the drinking locales

a muletear los argumentos
como si entraran a matar;
y acodados en los mostradores,
que simulan barreras,
brindan a la concurrencia
el miura disecado
que asoma la cabeza en la pared.

Ceñidos en sus capas, como toreros,
los curas entran en las peluquerías
a afeitarse en cuatrocientos espejos a la vez,
y cuando salen a la calle
ya tienen una barba de tres días.

En los invernáculos
edificados por los círculos,
la pereza se da como en ninguna parte
y los socios la ingieren
con churros o con horchata,
para encallar en los sillones
sus abulias y sus laxitudes de fantoches.

Cada doscientos cuarenta y siete hombres,
trescientos doce curas
y doscientos noventa y tres soldados,
pasa una mujer.

Sevilla, abril 1923.

waving arguments like red capes
as if they were going in for the kill;
and, elbows on the counters
that resemble sidelines,
they toast their audience
the stuffed Miura
that shows its head on the wall.

Capes clinging to them like bullfighters,
priests head to the barbershops
to be shaved in four hundred mirrors at once,
and the moment they step out on the street
they've already sprouted a three-day beard.

In hothouses
built by the social clubs
idleness is common like nowhere else
and the members drink it in
with churros or horchata,
they run aground in their armchairs
with indifference and puppet-like slackness.

Once every two hundred forty-seven men,
three hundred twelve priests
and two hundred ninety-three soldiers,
a woman goes by.

Seville, April 1923

EL TREN EXPRESO

A D. Gabriel Alomar.

Los vagones resbalan
sobre los trastes de la vía,
para cantar en sus dos cuerdas
la reciedumbre del paisaje.

Campos de piedra,
donde las vides sacan
una mano amenazante
de bajo tierra.

Jamelgos que llevan
una vida de asceta,
con objeto de entrar
en la plaza de toros.

Chanchos enloquecidos de flacura
que se creen una Salomé
porque tienen las nalgas muy rosadas.

Sobre la cresta de los peñones,
vestidas de primera comunión,
las casas de los aldeanos se arrodillan

EXPRESS TRAIN

To D. Gabriel Alomar

The carriages slide
over the frets of the tracks
to sing on their two strings
the landscape's grit.

Fields of stone,
where vines shoot
a menacing hand
out of the earth.

Nags who lead
ascetic lives
aiming to enter
the bullring.

Haggard hogs gone mad
who think they are Salomé
because their hams are so rosy.

On the crest of the crag,
dressed for First Communion,
the villagers' houses kneel

a los pies de la iglesia,
se aprietan unas a otras,
la levantan
como si fuera una custodia,
se anestesian de siesta
y de repiqueteo de campana.

A riesgo de que el viaje termine para siempre,
la locomotora hace pasar las piedras
a diez y seis kilómetros
y cuando ya no puede más,
se detiene, jadeante.

A veces "suele" acontecer
que precisamente allí
se encuentra una estación.

¡Campanas! ¡Silbidos! ¡Gritos!;
y el maquinista, que se despide siete veces
del jefe de la estación;
y el loro, que es el único pasajero que protesta
por las catorce horas de retardo;
y las chicas que vienen a ver pasar el tren
porque es lo único que pasa.

De repente,
los vagones resbalan
sobre los trastes de la vía,
para cantar en sus dos cuerdas
la reciedumbre del paisaje.

at the foot of the church,
they press together,
they lift it
as if it were a monstrance,
they are anesthetized by siesta
and the tintinnabulation of bells.

At the risk that the trip will end for good,
the locomotive propels the stones
at sixteen kilometers per hour
and when it can't go on any longer
it stops, panting.

Sometimes, it "usually" happens
that a station
is precisely there.

Bells! Whistles! Shouts!;
and the engine driver, who says goodbye
to the station chief seven times;
and the parrot, who is the only passenger to protest
the fourteen-hour delay;
and the girls who come to see the train pass
because it is the only thing that comes to pass.

Suddenly,
the carriages slide
over the frets of the tracks
to sing on their two strings
the landscape's grit.

Campos de piedra,
donde las vides sacan
una mano amenazante
de bajo tierra.

Jamelgos que llevan
una vida de asceta,
con objeto de entrar
en la plaza de toros.

Chanchos enloquecidos de flacura
que se creen una Salomé
porque tienen las nalgas muy rosadas.

En los compartimentos de primera,
las butacas nos atornillan sus elásticos
y nos descorchan un riñón,
en tanto que las arañas
realizan sus ejercicios de bombero
alrededor de la lamparilla
que se incendia en el techo.

A riesgo de que el viaje termine para siempre,
la locomotora hace pasar las piedras
a diez y seis kilómetros,
y cuando ya no puede más,
se detiene, jadeante.

¿Llegaremos al alba,
o mañana al atardecer . . . ?

Fields of stone,
where vines shoot
a menacing hand
out of the earth.

Nags who lead
ascetic lives
aiming to enter
the bullring.

Haggard hogs gone mad
who think they are Salomé
because their hams are so rosy.

In the first-class compartments,
the seats screw springs into us
and uncork our kidneys,
while spiders
practice their fireman exercises
around the lamp
that burns on the ceiling.

At the risk that the trip will end for good,
the locomotive propels the stones past
at sixteen kilometers per hour
and when it can't go on any longer
it stops, panting.

Will we arrive at dawn,
or tomorrow evening . . . ?

A través de la borra de las ventanillas,
el crepúsculo espanta
a los rebaños de sombras
que salen de abajo de las rocas
mientras nos vamos sepultando
en una luz de catacumba.

Se oye:
el canto de las mujeres
que mondan las legumbres
del puchero de pasado mañana;
el ronquido de los soldados
que, sin saber por qué,
nos trae la seguridad
de que se han sacado los botines;
los números del extracto de lotería,
que todos los pasajeros aprenden de memoria,
pues en los kioscos no han hallado
ninguna otra cosa para leer.

¡Si al menos pudiéramos arrimar un ojo
a alguno de los agujeritos que hay en el cielo!

¡Campanas! ¡Silbidos! ¡Gritos!;
y el maquinista, que se despide siete veces
del jefe de la estación;
y el loro, que es el único pasajero que protesta
por las veintisiete horas de retardo;
y las chicas que vienen a ver pasar el tren
porque es lo único que pasa.

Through the grimy windows
dusk scares off
flocks of shadows
that creep out from the rocks
while we go on burying ourselves
in catacomb light.

You can hear:
the song of women
peeling stew vegetables
for the day after tomorrow;
the snore of soldiers,
which assures us,
without knowing why,
that they've taken their boots off;
the numbers of the lottery summary
which all the passengers learn by heart
since they haven't found anything else
to read at the newsstands.

If we could have at least cozied an eye
up to one of those pinholes in the sky!

Bells! Whistles! Shouts!;
and the engine driver, who says goodbye
to the station chief seven times;
and the parrot, who is the only passenger to protest
the twenty-seven-hour delay;
and the girls who come to see the train pass
because it is the only thing that comes to pass.

De repente,
los vagones resbalan
sobre los trastes de la vía,
para cantar en sus dos cuerdas
la reciedumbre del paisaje.

¿España? ¿1870? . . . ¿1923? . . .

Suddenly,
the carriages slide
over the frets of the tracks
to sing on their two strings
the landscape's grit.

                                        Spain? 1870? . . . 1923? . . .

GIBRALTAR

El peñón enarca
su espinazo de tigre
que espera dar un zarpazo
en el canal.

Agarradas a la única calle,
como a una amarra,
las casas hacen equilibrio
para no caerse al mar,
donde los malecones
arrullan entre sus brazos
a los buques de guerra,
que tienen epidermis y letargos de cocodrilo.

Las caras idénticas
a esas esculturas
que los presidiarios tallan
en un carozo de aceituna,
los indios venden
marfiles de tibias de mamut,
sedas auténticas de Munich,
juegos de té,
que las señoras ocultan bajo sus faldas,

GIBRALTAR

The rock arches
its tigerish backbone
waiting to take a swipe
at the channel.

Gripping the single street
like a mooring,
the houses balance
so as not to fall into the sea
where, in their arms,
the breakwaters
lull dreadnoughts
which have the skin and lethargy of a crocodile.

Their faces identical
to the sculptures
convicts carve
in olive pits,
Indians sell
mamut shinbone ivory,
authentic Munich silk,
tea sets,
which the ladies hide in their skirts,

con objeto de abanicar su azoramiento
al cruzar la frontera.

Hartos de tierra firme,
las marineros
se embarcan en los cafés,
hasta que el mareo los zambulle
bajo las mesas,
o tocan a rebato
con las campanas de sus pantalones
para que las niñeras
acudan a agravar
sus nostalgias, de países lejanos,
con que las pipas inciensan
las veredas de la ciudad.

Algeciras, febrero 1923.

in order to fan their agitation
when they cross the border.

Fed up with terra firma,
the sailors
board cafés,
until queasiness dunks them
under tables,
or their bellbottoms
sound the alarm
so that nursemaids
deepen their nostalgia
for distant countries,
which pipes then waft
over the city sidewalks.

Algeciras, February 1923

TÁNGER

A D. Alfonso Maseras.

La hélice deja de latir;
así las casas no se vuelan,
como una bandada de gaviotas.

Erizadas de manos y de brazos
que emergen de unas mangas enormes,
las barcas de los nativos nos abordan
para que, en alaridos de gorila,
ellos irrumpan en cubierta
y emprendan con fardos y valijas
un partido de "rugby".

Sobre el muelle de desembarco,
que, desde lejos,
es un parral rebosante de uvas negras,
los hombres, al hablar,
hacen los mismos gestos
que si tocaran un "jazz-band",
y cuando quedan en silencio
provocan la tentación
de echarles una moneda en la tetilla
y hundirles de una trompada el esternón.

TANGIER

To D. Alfonso Maseras

The propeller stops pulsing;
so the houses don't fly off
like a flock of seagulls.

Bristling with hands and arms
that emerge from enormous sleeves,
the natives' boats board us
so that, with gorilla shrieks,
they erupt onto the deck
and strike up a *rugby* game
with bundles and suitcases.

On the landing dock,
which, from afar,
is a vineyard brimming with black grapes,
men, when they speak,
use the same gestures they would
if they played in a *jazz-band*,
and when they fall silent
they provoke the temptation
to toss a coin at their nipple
and sink their sternums with a blow.

Calles que suben,
titubean,
se adelgazan
para poder pasar,
se agachan bajo las casas,
se detienen a tomar sol,
se dan de narices
contra los clavos de las puertas
que les cierran el paso.

¡Calles que muerden los pies
a cuantos no los tienen achatados
por las travesías del desierto!

A caballo en los lomos de sus mamás,
los chicos les taconean la verija
para que no se dejen alcanzar
por los burros que pasan
con las ancas ensangrentadas
de palos y de erres.

Cada ochocientos metros
de mal olor
nos hace "flotar"
de un "upper-cut".

Fantasmas en zapatillas,
que nos miran con sus ojos desnudos,
las mujeres
entran en zaguanes tan frescos y azulados
que los hubiera firmado Fray Angélico,
se detienen ante las tiendas,

Streets that climb,
hesitate,
make themselves thin
to squeeze by,
crouch under the houses,
pause to get some sun,
bump smack into
the doornails
that block their way.

Streets that bite the feet
of the few whose aren't flattened
by desert crossings!

Mounted on the backs of their mamas,
kids tap their flanks
so that they won't be overtaken
by the burros going by
haunches bloodied
by sticks and stubbornness.

Every eight hundred meters
of stench
makes us "float"
from an "uppercut."

Ghosts in slippers
who watch us with their naked eyes,
the women
enter the hallways as fresh and bluish
as if signed by Fray Angelico,
they pause in front of the stores,

donde los mercaderes,
como en un relicario,
ensayan posturas budescas
entre las nubes tormentosas
de sus pipas de "kiff".

Con dos ombligos en los ojos
y una telaraña en los sobacos,
los pordioseros petrifican
una mueca de momia;
ululan lamentaciones
con sus labios de perro,
o una quejumbre de "cante hondo";
inciensan de tragedia las calles
al reproducir sobre los muros
votivas actitudes de estela.

En el pequeño zoco,
las diligencias automóviles,
¡guardabarros con olor a desierto!,
ábranse paso entre una multitud
que negocia en todas las lenguas de Babel,
arroja y abaraja los vocablos
como si fueran clavas,
se los arranca de la boca
como si se extrajera los molares.

Impermeables a cuanto las rodea,
las inglesas pasean en los burros,
sin tan siquiera emocionarse
ante el gesto con que los vendedores
abren sus dos alas de alfombras:

where the merchants,
as in a reliquary,
practice Buddhesque poses
among the storm clouds
of their *kiff* pipes.

With two navels in their eyes
and a spider web in their armpits,
the beggars petrify
a mummy's grimace;
ululate a lamentation
with their dog lips,
or a whine of *cante hondo*;
they waft the streets with tragedy
when they copy onto the walls
the votive attitudes of a stele.

In the little souk,
the horseless carriage—
fender smelling of desert!—
parts the crowd
that negotiates in all the languages of Babel,
spews and sloshes vowels
like scuppers,
extracts them from its mouth
like molars.

Impervious to their surroundings,
the English women go for a burro ride,
not the least bit moved
by the gesture with which the vendors
flap their two wings of carpet:

gesto de mariposa enferma
que no puede volar.

Chaquets de cucaracha,
sonrisas bíblicas,
dedos de ave de rapiña,
los judíos realizan la paradoja de vender
el dinero con que los otros compran;
y cargados de leña y de jorobas
los dromedarios arriban
con una escupida de desprecio
hacia esa humanidad que gesticula
hasta con las orejas,
vende hasta las uñas de los pies.

¡Barrio de panaderos
que estudian para diablo!
¡Barrio de zapateros
que al rematar cada puntada
levantan los brazos
en un simulacro de naufragio!
¡Barrio de peluqueros
que mondan las cabezas como papas
y extraen a cada cliente
un vasito de "sherry-brandy" del cogote!

Desde lo alto de los alminares
los almuédanos,
al ver caer el Sol,
instan a lavarse los pies

gesture of a sick butterfly
unable to take flight.

Cockroach tailcoats,
biblical smiles,
bird-of-prey fingers,
Jews accomplish the paradox of selling
the money that other people use to buy things;
and burdened by wood and humps
the camels arrive
with a spit of disdain
for this humanity that gestures
even with its ears,
sells even its toenails.

Neighborhood of bakers
who study to become devils!
Neighborhood of cobblers
who, when they finish each stitch,
lift their arms
in sham shipwreck!
Neighborhood of hairdressers
who peel heads like potatoes
and extract, from the nape
of every client's neck,
a dram of *sherry-brandy*!

From the top of the minarets
the muezzins,
when they see the sun set,
urge the faithful
to wash their feet,

a los fieles, que acuden
con las cabezas vendadas
cual si los hubieran trepanado.

Y de noche,
cuando la vida de la ciudad
trepa las escaleras de gallinero
de los café-conciertos,
el ritmo entrecortado
de las flautas y del tambor
hieratiza las posturas egipcias
con que los hombres recuéstanse en los muros,
donde penden alfanjes de zarzuela
y el Kaiser abraza en las litografías al Sultán . . .

En tanto que, al resplandor lunar,
las palmeras que emergen de los techos
semejan arañas fabulosas
colgadas del cielo raso de la noche.

Tánger, mayo 1923.

they who arrive
with their heads bandaged
as if they had been trepanned.

And at night,
when city life
climbs the henhouse stairs
of café-concerts,
the fitful rhythm
of flutes and drum
englyphs the Egyptian postures
of men leaning against walls
where hang *zarzuela* scimitars
and lithographs
of the Kaiser embracing the Sultan . . .

While, in the lunar gleam,
palm trees that emerge from roofs
resemble fabulous spiders
suspended from the clear night sky.

Tangier, May 1923

SIESTA

Un zumbido de moscas anestesia la aldea.
El sol unta con fósforo el frente de las casas,
y en el cauce reseco de las calles que sueñan
deambula un blanco espectro vestido de caballo.

Penden de los balcones racimos de glicinas
que agravan el aliento sepulcral de los patios
al insinuar la duda de que acaso estén muertos
los hombres y los niños que duermen en el suelo.

La bondad soñolienta que trasudan las cosas
se expresa en las pupilas de un burro que trabaja
y en las ubres de madre de las cabras que pasan
con un son de cencerros que, al diluirse en la tarde,
no se sabe si aún suena o ya es sólo un recuerdo . . .
¡Es tan real el paisaje que parece fingido!

Andalusia, 1923.

116

SIESTA

The buzzing of flies anesthetizes the village.
The sun butters the house fronts with phosphorous,
and in the dry riverbed of the streets that dream
a white specter wanders dressed as a horse.

From the balconies hang bunches of wisteria
that pollute the patios' sepulchral breath
by suggesting that the men and children
asleep on the floor may be dead.

The somnolent goodness that things sweat out
expressed in the pupils of a laboring burro
and in the mammaries of goats going by
with the chime of cowbells that, as they dissolve in the afternoon,
make it hard to know if they're still ringing or if it's just a memory . . .
How real, the landscape that looks fake!

Andalusia, 1923

JUERGA

A D. Eugenio d'Ors.

Los frescos pintados en la pared
transforman el "Salón Reservado"
en una "Plaza de Toros", donde el suelo
tiene la consistencia y el color de la "arena":
gracias a que todas las noches
se riega la tierra con jerez.

Jinetes en sillas esqueletosas,
tufos planchados con saliva,
una estrella clavada en la corbata,
otra en el dedo meñique,
los tertulianos exigen que el "cantaor"
lamente el retardo de las mujeres
con ¡ayes! que lo retuercen
en calambres de indigestión.

De pronto,
en un sobresalto de pavor,
la cortina deja pasar seis senos
que aportan tres "mamás".

Los párpados como dos castañuelas,
las pupilas como dos cajas de betún,

CAROUSAL

To D. Eugenio d'Ors

The frescoes painted on the wall
transform the "Reserved Salon"
into a "Bullring," where the floor
has the consistency and color of "sand":
because every night
the ground is watered with sherry.

Jockeys in skeletal chairs,
curls smoothed down with spit,
stars pinned to their ties
and to their pinkies,
the partygoers implore the "flamenco" singer
to lament the ladies' lateness
with ays! that make him writhe
with stomach cramps.

Abruptly,
with a terrified twitch,
the curtain lets six breasts pass
carried by three "mamas."

Eyelids like two castanets,
pupils like two tins of shoe polish,

negro el pelo,
negras las pestañas
y las extremidades de las uñas,
las siguen cuatro "niñas", que al entrar,
provocan una descarga de ¡olés!
que desmaya a las ratas que transitan el corredor.

La servilleta a guisa de "capote",
el camarero lidia el humo de los cigarros
y la voracidad de la clientela,
con "pases" y chuletas "al natural",
o "entra" a "colocar" el sacacorchos
como "pone" su vara un picador.

Abroqueladas en armaduras medievales,
en el casco flamea la bandera de España,
las botellas de manzanilla
se agotan al combatir a los chorizos
que mugen en los estómagos,
o sangran en los platos
como toros lidiados.

Previa autorización de las "mamás",
las "niñas" van a sentarse
sobre las rodillas de los hombres,
para cambiar un beso por un duro,
mientras el "cantaor",
muslos de rana
embutidos en fundas de paraguas,
tartamudea una copla
que lo desinfla nueve kilos.

hair, black
eyelashes, black
and fingernail tips
follow four "girls" who as they enter
provoke such a volley of *olés!*
that passing rats pass out in the hallway.

A napkin draped like a "cape,"
the waiter contends with the cigarette smoke
and a voracious clientele
with "passes" and "natural" pork chop sideburns,
or "enters" to "place" the corkscrew
just as a picador "places" his lance.

Encased in medieval armor,
the Spanish flag blazing from their helmets,
the manzanilla bottles
are drained from combat with chorizos
that bellow in stomachs
or bleed on plates
like embattled bulls.

With prior authorization from the "mamas,"
the "girls" go sit
on men's knees,
to exchange a kiss for a coin,
while the "flamenco" singer,
frog thighs
stuffed in umbrella covers,
stammers a *copla*
that deflates him by nine kilos.

Los brazos en alto,
desnudas las axilas,
así dan un pregusto de sus intimidades,
las "niñas" menean, luego, las caderas
como si alguien se las hiciera dar vueltas por adentro,
y en húmedas sonrisas de extenuación,
describen con sus pupilas
las parabólicas trayectorias de un espasmo,
que hace gruñir de deseo
hasta a los espectadores pintados en la pared.

Después de semejante simulacro
ya nadie tiene fuerza ni para hacer rodar
las bolitas de pan, ensombrecidas,
entre las yemas de los dedos.

Poco a poco, la luz aséptica de la mañana
agrava los ayes del "cantaor"
hasta identificar
la palidez trasnochada de los rostros
con la angustiosa resignación
de una clientela de dentista.

Se oye el "klaxon" que el sueño hace sonar
en las jetas de las "mamás",
los suspiros del "cantaor"
que abraza en la guitarra
una nostalgia de mujer,
los cachetazos con que las "niñas"
persuaden a los machos
que no hay nada que hacer

Arms raised,
bared pits
giving a foretaste of their privates,
the "girls" then wiggle their hips
as if someone spun them from inside,
and with damp smiles of exhaustion,
their pupils trace
spasmodic parabolic trajectories,
so that even the spectators painted on the walls
groan with desire.

After such a simulation
no one even has the strength to roll
darkening crumbs of bread
between their fingertips.

Little by little, the morning's aseptic light
deepens the ays of the "flamenco" singer
until it identifies
the sleepless pallor of faces
with the anxious resignation
of a dentist's patient.

You can hear the "klaxon" that the dream sounds
in the mugs of the "mamas,"
the sighs of the "flamenco" singer
who holds in his guitar
his nostalgia for a woman,
the slaps with which the "girls"
persuade the males
there's nothing to do

sino dejarlas en su casa,
y sepultarse en la abstinencia
de las camas heladas.

Madrid, 1923.

but drop them off at home,
and bury themselves in the abstinence
of their icy beds.

Madrid, 1923

ESCORIAL

A D. José Ortega y Gasset.

A medida que nos aproximamos
las piedras se van dando mejor.

Desnudo, anacorético,
las ventanas idénticas entre sí,
como la vida de sus monjes,
el Escorial levanta sus muros de granito
por los que no treparán nunca los mandingas,
pues ni aún dentro de novecientos años.
hallarán una arruga donde hincar
sus pezuñas de azufre y pedernal.

Paradas en lo alto de las chimeneas,
las cigüeñas meditan la responsabilidad
de ser la única ornamentación del monasterio,
mientras el viento que reza en las rendijas
ahuyenta las tentaciones que amenazan
entrar por el tejado.

Cencerro de las piedras que pastan
en los alrededores,
las campanas de la iglesia
espantan a los ángeles

ESCORIAL

To D. José Ortega y Gasset

The stones keep getting better
as we approach.

Naked, anchoritic,
the windows as identical to one another
as the lives of its monks,
the Escorial raises its granite walls
so the devils will never clamber up it,
not even in nine hundred years
will they discover a crease in which to sink
their hooves of sulfur and flint.

Standing atop the chimneys,
storks contemplate the responsibility
of being the monastery's sole ornamentation,
while the wind praying in the cracks
frightens off the temptations that threaten
to enter through the roof tiles.

Cowbell of stones that graze
around the monastery,
the church bells
scare the angels

que viven en su torre
y suelen tomarlos de improviso,
haciéndoles perder alguna pluma
sobre el adoquinado de los patios.

¡Corredores donde el silencio tonifica
la robustez de las columnas!
¡Salas donde la austeridad es tan grande,
que basta una sonrisa de mujer
para que nos asedien los pecados de "Bosch"
y sólo se desbanden en retirada
al advertir que nuestro guía
es nuestro propio arcángel,
que se ha disfrazado de guardián!

Los visitantes,
la cabeza hundida entre los hombros
(así la Muerte no los podrá agarrar
como se agarra a un gato),
descienden a las tumbas y al pudridero,
y al salir,
perciben el esqueleto de la gente
con la misma facilidad
con que antes les distinguían la nariz.

Cuando una luna fantasmal
nieva su luz en las techumbres,
los ruidos de las inmediaciones
adquieren psicologías criminales,
y el silencio
alcanza tal intensidad,
que se camina

that live in its tower
and tend to take them by surprise,
causing them to shed a feather
on the cobblestoned patios.

Corridors where the silence invigorates
the columns' robustness!
Halls of such great austerity
that a woman's smile is enough
for the sins of Bosch to besiege us
and only beat a retreat
when they notice that our guide
is our own Archangel
disguised as a guard!

The visitors,
heads sunk between their shoulders
(so that Death won't catch them
as one catches a cat),
descend to the tombs and the decaying chamber,
and as they exit,
they perceive people's skeletons
just as easily
as they once discerned their noses.

When a ghostly moon
snows its light over the rooftops
the noises of the vicinity
take on criminal psychologies,
and the silence
reaches such an intensity
that it falls

como si se entrara en un concierto,
y se contienen las ganas de toser
por temor a que el eco repita nuestra tos
hasta convencernos de que estamos tuberculosos.

¡Horas en que los perros se enloquecen de soledad
y en las que el miedo
hace girar las cabezas de las lechuzas y de los hombres,
quienes, al enfrentarnos,
se persignan bajo el embozo
por si nosotros fuéramos Satán!

Escorial, abril 1923.

as if entering a concert,
and the desire to cough is suppressed
for fear that our cough will echo
until it convinces us we are consumptives.

Times when dogs go mad from solitude
and when fear
turns the heads of owls and men
who, when they face us,
cross themselves beneath their cloaks
just in case we are Satan!

Escorial, April 1923

ALHAMBRA

A Margarita Nelken.

Los surtidores pulverizan
una lasitud
que apenas nos deja meditar
con los poros, el cerebelo y la nariz.

¡Estanques de absintio
en los que se remojan
los encajes de piedra de los arcos!

¡Alcobas en las que adquiere la luz
la dulzura y la voluptuosidad
que adquiere la luz
en una boca entreabierta de mujer!

Con una locuacidad de Celestina,
los guías
conducen a las mujeres al harén,
para que se ruboricen escuchando
lo que las fuentes les cuentan al pasar,
y para que, asomadas al Albaicín,
se enfermen de "saudades"
al oír la muzárabe canción,

ALHAMBRA

To Margarita Nelken

The fountains pulverize
a lassitude
that scarcely lets us meditate
with our pores, cerebellum, and nose.

The stone lace of the arches
soaks
in absinthe ponds!

Alcoves where light acquires
the sweet sensuousness
that light acquires
in a woman's half-open mouth!

With all the loquacity of Celestina,
guides
lead women to the harem,
making them blush when they hear
what the fountains recount as they pass,
and so that, leaning out of the Albaicín,
they fall ill from *saudades*
when they hear the Mozarabic song

que todavía la ciudad
sigue tocando con sordina.

Cuellos y ademanes de mamboretá,
las inglesas componen sus paletas
con el gris de sus pupilas londinenses
y la desesperación encarnada de ser vírgenes,
y como si se miraran al espejo,
reproducen,
con exaltaciones de tarjeta postal,
las estancias llenas de una nostalgia de cojines
y de sombras violáceas, como ojeras.

En el mirador de Lindaraja,
los visitantes se estremecen al comprobar
que las columnas
tienen la blancura y el grosor
de los brazos de la favorita,
y en el departamento de los baños
se suenan la nariz
con el intento de catar
ese olor a carne de odalisca,
carne que tiene una consistencia y un sabor
de pastilla de goma.

¡Persianas patinadas
por todos los ojos
que han mirado al través!

¡Paredes que bajo sus camisas de puntilla
tienen treinta y siete grados a la sombra!

that the city just
keeps on playing with a damper.

With the necks and expressions of mantises,
the English ladies compose their palettes
with their London-gray pupils
and the incarnate desperation of their virginity,
as if looking in the mirror,
they reproduce,
in postcard exaltations,
sojourns full of nostalgia for cushions
and shadows as violet as rings under the eyes.

From the windowed balcony of Lindaraja,
the visitors shudder, confirming
that the columns
have the whiteness and thickness
of the favorite's arms,
and in the bathhousees
they blow their noses
in hopes of sampling
that scent of Odalisque flesh,
flesh that has the taste and feel
of fruit pastilles.

Venetian blinds polished
by all the eyes
that have looked through them!

Walls that, under their lace-embroidered blouses,
are thirty-seven degrees in the shade!

Decididamente,
cada vez que salimos
del Alhambra
es como si volviéramos
de una cita de amor.

Clearly,
every time we leave
the Alhambra
it's as if we were returning
from a hot date.

Granada, March 1923

SEMANA SANTA

A Miguel Ángel del Pino,
que, con una exquisita amabilidad sevillana,
inicióme en los complicados ritos de la más
bella fiesta popular.

Vísperas

Desde el amanecer, se cambia la ropa sucia de los altares y de los santos, que huele a rancia bendición, mientras los plumeros inciensan una nube de polvo tan espesa, que las arañas apenas hallan tiempo de levantar sus redes de equilibrista, para ir a ajustarlas en los barrotes de la cama del sacristán.

Con todas las características del criminal nato lombrosiano, los apóstoles se evaden de sus nichos, ante las vírgenes atónitas, que rompen a llorar . . . porque no viene el peluquero a ondularles las crenchas.

Enjutos, enflaquecidos de insomnio y de impaciencia, los nazarenos pruébanse el capirote cada cinco minutos, o llegan, acompañados de un amigo, a presentarle la virgen, como si fuera su querida.

Ya no queda por alquilar ni una cornisa desde la que se vea pasar la procesión.

HOLY WEEK

To Miguel Ángel del Pino,
who, with exquisite Sevillian kindness,
introduced me to the complicated rites of the most
beautiful popular holiday.

Vespers

Since dawn, they've been changing the altars and the saints' dirty laundry, which smells of stale benediction, while feather dusters waft a cloud of dust so thick that the spiders scarcely find time to lift their tightrope walker's webs and fit them into the crosspieces of the sacristan's bed.

With all the attributes of a Lombrosian-born criminal, the apostles flee their niches before the astonished virgins, who burst into tears . . . because the hairdresser isn't coming to set their curls.

Gaunt, grown thin from insomnia and impatience, the Nazarenes try on the conical hat every five minutes; or they arrive, accompanied by a friend, to greet the virgin as if she were their beloved.

You can't even rent a cornice anymore to watch the procession go by.

Minuto tras minuto va cayendo sobre la ciudad una manga de ingleses con una psicología y una elegancia de langosta.

A vista de ojo, los hoteleros engordan ante la perspectiva de doblar la tarifa.

Llega un cuerpo del ejército de Marruecos, expresamente para sacar los candelabros y la custodia del tesoro.

Frente a todos los espejos de la ciudad, las mujeres ensayan su mirada "Smith Wesson"; pues, como las vírgenes, sólo salen de casa esta semana, y si no cazan nada, seguirán siéndolo . . .

Domingo de Ramos (mañana)

¡Campanas!
¡Repiqueteo de campanas!
¡Campanas con café con leche!
¡Campanas que nos imponen una cadencia al abrocharnos los botines!
¡Campanas que acompasan el paso de la gente que pasa en las aceras!
¡Campanas!
¡Repiqueteo de campanas!

En la catedral, el rito se complica tanto, que los sacerdotes necesitan apuntador.

Trece siglos de ensayos permiten armonizar las florecencias de las rejas con el contrapaso de los monaguillos y la caligrafía del misal.

Una luz de "Museo Grevin" dramatiza la mirada vidriosa de los cristos, ahonda la voz de los prelados que cantan, se interrogan y se

Minute after minute English swarms descend on the city with the psychology and elegance of locusts.

Catching a glimpse, the hoteliers puff up at the prospect of doubling their prices.

The Moroccan Army Corps appears, specifically to take the candelabras and custody of the treasure.

At every mirror in the city, the women try out their *Smith Wesson* look; and like the virgins, they only leave the house this week, and if they don't hunt anything down, they will remain virgins . . .

Palm Sunday (morning)

Bells!
Pealing of bells!
Bells with *café con leche*!
Bells impose a cadence on us as we buckle our boots!
Bells keep step with people who step along the sidewalk's stepping stones!
Bells!
Pealing of bells!

In the cathedral, the rite gets so complicated that the priests need a prompter.

Thirteen centuries of rehearsals allow the grille-works' bloom to harmonize with the altar boys' *contrapaso* and the missal's calligraphy.

A "Grevin Museum" light dramatizes the Christs' glassy gaze, deepens the voice of the prelates who sing, question, and answer, like those

contestan, como esos sapos con vientre de prelado, una boca predestinada a engullir hostias y las manos enfermas de reumatismo, por pasarse las noches—de cuclillas en el pantano—cantando a las estrellas.

Si al repartir las palmas no interviniera una fuerza sobrenatural, los feligreses aplaudirían los rasos con que la procesión sale a la calle, donde el obispo—con sus ochenta kilos de bordados—bate el "record" de dar media vuelta a la manzana y entra nuevamente en escena, para que continúe la función . . .

(tarde)

¡Agua!
¡Agüita fresca!
¿Quién quiere agua?

En un flujo y reflujo de espaldas y de brazos, los acorazados de los cacahueteros fondean entre la multitud, que espera la salida de los "pasos" haciendo "pan francés".

Espantada por los flagelos de papel, la codicia de los pilletes revolotea y zumba en torno a las canastas de pasteles, mientras los nazarenos sacian la sed, que sentirán, en tabernas que expenden borracheras garantizadas por toda la semana.

Sin asomar las narices a la calle, los santos realizan el milagro de que los balcones no se caigan.

¡Agua!
¡Agüita fresca!

toads with a prelate's belly, mouth foreordained to gobble down hosts and hands sick with rheumatism, from nights spent—squatting in a swamp—singing to the stars.

If, as palm leaves are passed around, no supernatural force were to intervene, the parishioners would applaud the speed of the procession heading into the street, where the bishop—with his eighty kilos of embroidery—breaks the "record" for going halfway around the block and reenters the scene: for the show must go on . . .

(afternoon)

Water!
Agüita fresca!
Who wants water?

In the ebb and flow of backs and arms, the peanut vendors' dreadnoughts anchor amid the crowd awaiting the floats to come out making French bread.

Frightened by the paper whips, the urchins' greed hovers and buzzes around the pastry baskets, while Nazarenes quench their thirst, which they will regret, in taverns peddling drunkenness guaranteed to last all week.

Without poking their heads into the street, the saints perform the miracle of preventing the balconies from collapsing.

Water!
Agüita fresca!

¿Quién quiere agua?
pregonan los aguateros al servirnos una reverencia de minué.

De repente, las puertas de la iglesia se abren como las de una esclusa, y, entre una doble fila de nazarenos que canaliza la multitud, una virgen avanza hasta las candilejas de su paso, constelada de joyas, como una cupletista.

Los espectadores, contorsionados por la emoción, arráncanse la chaquetilla y el sombrero, se acalambran en posturas de capeador, braman piropos que los nazarenos intentan acallar como el apagador que les oculta la cabeza.

Cuando el Señor aparece en la puerta, las nubes se envuelven con un crespón, bajan hasta la altura de los techos, y, al verlo cogido como un torero, todas, unánimemente, comienzan a llorar.

¡Agua!
¡Agüita fresca!
¿Quién quiere agua?

Miércoles Santo

Las tribunas y las sillas colocadas enfrente del Ayuntamiento progresivamente se van ennegreciendo, como un pegamoscas de cocina.

Antes que la caballería comience a desfilar, los guardias civiles despejan la calzada, por temor a que los cachetes de algún trompa estallen como una bomba de anarquista.

Los caballos—la boca enjabonada cual si se fueran a afeitar—tienen

Who wants water?
hawk the water vendors, bowing as if dancing a minuet.

Suddenly, the church doors swing open like floodgates, and amid a double file of Nazarenes that channels the crowd, a virgin advances toward the footlights of her float, constellated with jewels like a coupletist.

The spectators, contorted with emotion, tear off their jackets and hats, strike a *capeador*'s cramped pose, bellowing *piropos* the Nazarenes try to silence like the candle extinguishers that hide their heads.

When the Lord appears in the doorway, the clouds wrap themselves in black crêpe, descend to the rooftops and, seeing him tossed like a bullfighter, they all, unanimously, begin to cry.

Water!
Agüita fresca!
Who wants water?

Spy Wednesday

The grandstand and the seats in front of City Hall grow progressively darker, like kitchen flytraps.

Before the cavalry begins to parade, the Civil Guard clears the carriageway, fearing some trumpet player's cheeks will explode like an anarchist's bomb.

The horses—their mouths lathered as though about to shave—have

las ancas tan lustrosas, que las mujeres aprovechan para arreglarse la mantilla y averiguar, sin darse vuelta, quién unta una mirada en sus caderas.

Con la solemnidad de un ejército de pingüinos, los nazarenos escoltan a los santos, que, en temblores de debutante, representan "misterios" sobre el tablado de las andas, bajo cuyos telones se divisan los pies de los "gallegos", tal como si cambiaran una decoración.

Pasa:
El Sagrado Prendimiento de Nuestro Señor, y Nuestra Señora del Dulce Nombre.
El Santísimo Cristo de las Siete Palabras, y María Santísima de los Remedios.
El Santísimo Cristo de las Aguas, y Nuestra Señora del Mayor Dolor.
La Santísima Cena Sacramental, y Nuestra Señora del Subterráneo.
El Santísimo Cristo del Buen Fin, y Nuestra Señora de la Palma.
Nuestro Padre Jesús atado a la Columna, y Nuestra Señora de las Lágrimas.
El Sagrado Descendimiento de Nuestro Señor, y La Quinta Angustia de María Santísima.

Y entre paso y paso:
¡Manzanilla! ¡Almendras garrapiñadas! ¡Jerez!

Estrangulados por la asfixia, los "gallegos" caen de rodillas cada cincuenta metros, y se resisten a continuar regando los adoquines de sudor, si antes no se les llena el tanque de aguardiente.

Cuando los nazarenos se detienen a mirarnos con sus ojos vacíos, irremisiblemente, algún balcón gargariza una "saeta" sobre la multitud,

haunches so lustrous the women take advantage of them to adjust their mantillas and to note, without turning around, whose glance honeys their hips.

With the solemnity of a penguin army, the Nazarenes escort the saints, who, trembling like debutants, perform their mysteries atop the float platforms, under whose curtains the feet of Galicians can be spotted as if they were changing a set.

Passing by:
The Sacred Arrest of Our Lord, and Our Lady of the Sweet Name.
Most Holy Christ of the Seven Words, and Most Holy Mary of the Cure.
Most Holy Christ of the Waters, and Our Lady of Greatest Sorrow.
Most Holy Sacramental Supper, and Our Lady of the Vault.
Most Holy Christ of Happy End, and Our Lady of the Palm.
Our Father Jesus tied to the Column, and Our Lady of Tears.
The Sacred Descent of Our Lord, and the Fifth Anguish of Most Holy Mary.

And between float and float:
Manzanilla! Candied almonds! Sherry!

Strangled by asphyxia, Galicians fall to their knees every fifty meters, and they refuse to keep watering the cobblestones with their sweat if their tank isn't first refilled with liquor.

As the Nazarenes pause to stare at us with their empty eyes, unforgivably, some balcony gargles a saeta over the crowd—frizzing into

encrespada en un ¡ole!, que estalla y se apaga sobre las cabezas, como si reventara en una playa.

Los penitentes cargados de una cruz desinflan el pecho de las mamás en un suspiro de neumático, apenas menos potente del que exhala la multitud al escaparse ese globito que siempre se le escapa a la multitud.

Todas las cofradías llevan un estandarte, donde se lee:

S. P. Q. R.

Jueves Santo

Es el día en que reciben todas las vírgenes de la ciudad.

Con la mantilla negra y los ojos que matan, las hembras repiquetean sus tacones sobre las lápidas de las aceras, se consternan al comprobar que no se derrumba ni una casa, que no resucita ningún Lázaro, y, cual si salieran de un toril, irrumpen en los atrios, donde los hombres les banderillean un par de miraduras, a riesgo de dejarse coger el corazón.

De pie en medio de la nave—dorada como un salón—, las vírgenes expiden su duelo en un sólido llanto de rubí, que embriaga la elocuencia de prospecto medicinal con que los hermanos ponderan sus encantos, cuando no optan por alzarles las faldas y persuadir a los espectadores de que no hay en el globo unas pantorrillas semejantes.

Después de la vigésima estación, si un fémur no nos ha perforado un intestino, contemplamos veintiocho "pasos" más, y acribillados de

an *olé!*—that bursts and fades over their heads as if crashing on a beach.

Cross-bearing penitents deflate mothers' breasts in a pneumatic sigh scarcely less powerful than the exhalation of the crowd when that little balloon escapes that always escapes from the crowd.

Each Brotherhood raises a standard that reads:

S. P. Q. R.

Maundy Thursday

It is the day when all the virgins of the city are welcomed.

With black mantilla and murderous eyes, the women's heels peal over the pavement stones, consternated to confirm that not one house has been razed, not one Lazarus raised, and, as if charging from a bullpen, they irrupt into the atria, where the men flag them with a glance or two, at the risk of getting their hearts gored.

Standing in the middle of the nave—gilded like a salon—the virgins issue their grief in a solid ruby wail, which inebriates the medically precise eloquence with which the monks praise their charms if the monks don't lift their skirts to persuade the spectators there are no comparable calves in all the world.

After the twentieth station, if a femur has not pierced an intestine, we'll ponder twenty-eight more floats, and riddled with saetas like

"saetas", como un San Sebastián, los pies desmenuzados como albóndigas, apenas tenemos fuerza para llegar hasta la puerta del hotel y desplomarnos entre los brazos de la levita del portero.

El "menú" nos hace volver en sí. Leemos, nos refregamos los ojos y volvemos a leer:

"Sopa de Nazarenos".
"Lenguado a la Pío X".

—¡Camarero! Un bife con papas.
—¿Con Papas, señor? . . .
—¡No, hombre!, con huevos fritos.

Madrugada y tarde del Viernes Santo.

Mientras se espera la salida del Cristo del Gran Poder, se reflexiona: en la superioridad del marabú, en la influencia de Goya sobre las sombras de los balcones, en la finura chinesca con que los árboles se esfuman en el azul nocturno.

Dos campanadas apagan luego los focos de la plaza; así, las espaldas se amalgaman hasta formar un solo cuerpo que sostiene de catorce a diez y nueve mil cabezas.

Con un ritmo siniestro de Edgar Poe—¡cirios rojos ensangrientan sus manos!—, los nazarenos perforan un silencio donde tan sólo se percibe el tic-tac de las pestañas, silencio desgarrado por "saetas" que escalofrían la noche y se vierten sobre la multitud como un líquido helado.

a Saint Sebastian, our feet crumbled like meatballs, we barely have the strength to make the hotel door and collapse in the arms of the porter's frock coat.

The very "menu" makes us come to. We read, rub our eyes, and read again:

—Soup of Nazarenes.
—Sole of Pious X.

"Waiter! I'll have a steak and fries."
"Friars, sir?"
"No man! . . . fried eggs."

Good Friday Dawn and Afternoon

While awaiting the departure of the Christ Almighty, you reflect: on the superiority of the marabou, on Goya's influence upon the balcony shadows, on the Chinese refinement of the trees blurring into nocturnal blue.

Then two chimes put out the plaza lights; in this way, backs amass until they form a single body that supports fourteen to nineteen thousand heads.

With a sinister Edgar Poe rhythm—red candles bloody their hands!—the Nazarenes pierce a silence where all that's heard is the tic-tac of eyelashes, a silence shot through with saetas that shiver the night and spill over the crowd like frozen liquid.

151

Seguido de cuatrocientas prostitutas arrepentidas del pecado menos original, el Cristo del Gran Poder camina sobre un oleaje de cabezas, que lo alza hasta el nivel de los balcones, en cuyos barrotes las mujeres aferran las ganas de tirarse a lamerle los pies.

En el resto de la ciudad el resplandor de los "pasos" ilumina las caras con una técnica de Rembrandt. Las sombras adquieren más importancia que los cuerpos, llevan una vida más aventurera y más trágica. La cofradía del "Silencio", sobre todo, proyecta en las paredes blancas un "film" dislocado y absurdo, donde las sombras trepan a los tejados, violan los cuartos de las hembras, se sepultan en los patios dormidos.

Entre "saetas" conservadas en aguardiente pasa la "Macarena", con su escolta romana, en cuyas corazas de latón se trasuntan los espectadores, alineados a lo largo de las aceras.

¡Es la hora de los churros y del anís!

Una luz sin fuerza para llegar al suelo ribetea con tiza las molduras y las aristas de las casas, que tienen facha de haber dormido mal, y obliga a salir de entre sus sábanas a las nubes desnudas, que se envuelven en gasas amarillentas y verdosas y se ciñen, por último, una túnica blanca.

Cuando suenan las seis, las cigüeñas ensayan un vuelo matinal, y tornan al campanario de la iglesia, a reanudar sus mansas divagaciones de burócrata jubilado.

Caras y actitudes de chimpancé, los presidiarios esperan, trepados en las rejas, que las vírgenes pasen por la cárcel antes de irse a dormir, para sollozar una "saeta" de arrepentimiento y de perdón, mientras

Followed by four hundred prostitutes repenting the least original sin, the Christ Almighty walks over a wave of heads, which raise him to balcony-level, in whose crosspieces the women restrain their desire to throw themselves down to lick his feet.

In the rest of the city the glare of the floats illuminates faces with Rembrandtesque technique. Shadows acquire more weight than bodies, they take on a more adventuresome, more tragic life. The Brotherhood of "Silence," over all, projects an absurd and dislocated "film" onto the white walls, where the shadows climb to the rooftops, trespass the females' rooms, and bury themselves in sleeping patios.

Between saetas preserved in liquor, the *Macarena* goes by with her Roman escort, in whose brass cuirass the spectators are duplicated as they line the length of the sidewalks.

It is time for churros and anise!

A light too weak to reach the ground limns the trim and molding of houses, which seem to have had a bad sleep, and compels the naked clouds to emerge from between the sheets, and wrap themselves in yellowish and greenish gases and lastly, cinch their white tunic.

When it strikes six, the storks attempt a morning flight and return to the church belfry, resuming the tame digressions of a retired bureaucrat.

With the faces and attitudes of chimpanzees, the convicts climbing the bars wait for the virgins to pass by the prison before going to sleep, to sob a saeta of repentance and forgiveness, while the Brotherhoods,

en bordejeos de fragata las cofradías que no han fondeado aún en las iglesias, encallan en todas las tabernas, abandonan sus vírgenes por la manzanilla y el jerez.

Ya en la cama, los nazarenos que nos transitan las circunvoluciones redoblan sus tambores en nuestra sien, y los churros, anidados en nuestro estómago, se enroscan y se anudan como serpientes.

Alguien nos destornilla luego la cabeza, nos desabrocha las costillas, intenta escamotearnos un riñón, al mismo tiempo que un insensato repique de campanas nos va sumergiendo en un sopor.

Después . . . ¿Han pasado semanas? ¿Han pasado minutos? . . . Una campanilla se desploma, como una sonda, en nuestro oído, nos iza a la superficie del colchón.

¡Apenas tenemos tiempo de alcanzar el entierro! . . .

¿Cuatrocientos setenta y ocho mil setecientos noventa y nueve "pasos" más?

¡Cristos ensangrentados como caballos de picador! ¡Cirios que nunca terminan de llorar! ¡Concejales que han alquilado un frac que enternece a las Magdalenas! ¡Cristos estirados en una lona de bombero que acaban de arrojarse de un balcón! ¡La Verónica y el Gobernador . . . con su escolta de arcángeles!

¡Y las centurias romanas . . . de Marruecos, y las Sibilas, y los Santos Varones! ¡Todos los instrumentos de la Pasión! . . . ¡Y el instrumento máximo, ¡la Muerte!, entronizada sobre el mundo . . . , que es un punto final!

in tightly tacking frigates that have yet to dock in the churches, run aground in every tavern, abandon their virgins for manzanilla and sherry.

Already in bed, the Nazarenes traversing our circumvolutions redouble their pounding in our temples, and the churros, nesting in our stomachs, coil and knot like snakes.

Then someone screws our heads loose, cracks our ribs, tries to palm a kidney, while at the same time a senseless peal of bells submerges us in a stupor.

Later . . . Has it been weeks? Has it been minutes? A bell drops down like a reckoning in our ear, hoisting us back to the mattress' surface.

We barely have time to get to the burial! . . .

Four hundred seventy-eight thousand seven hundred ninety-nine more floats?

Christs bloodied like a picador's horses! Candles that don't stop weeping! Councilmen with rented tailcoats that deeply move the Magdalenes! Christs, stretched out on a fireman's trampoline, having just flung themselves from a balcony! The Veronica and the Governor . . . with their escort of archangels!

And the Roman centurions . . . from Morocco, and the Sibyls, and the Holy Men! All the instruments of the Passion! And the maximum instrument, Death! enthroned above the world . . . which is a full stop!

¿Morir? ¡Señor! ¡Señor! ¡Libradnos, Señor!
¿Dormir? ¡Dormir! ¡Concedédnoslo, Señor!

Sevilla, mayo 1923.

To die? Lord! Lord! Free us, Lord!
To sleep? To sleep! Give us that, Lord!

Seville, May 1923

ACKNOWLEDGMENTS

This book would not be possible without the early collaboration of Gabriel Milner and the help of Pablo Palomino.

Susana Lange patiently supported this project for nearly a decade and offered several excellent suggestions for the translation. Jennifer Grotz kindly selected the book for Open Letter Books, for which we are deeply grateful. Heartfelt thanks to Kaija Straumanis and Chad Post for their commitment to bringing Argentine literature to English-speaking readers, and more broadly, for their tireless efforts to publish literature in translation.

Thanks to Alejandra Uslenghi and Susan Manning for testing these translations in their classrooms with the Northwestern University Kaplan Scholars in the course "The Avant-Garde in the World," and thanks to Ben Shear for his myriad conversations during his concurrent study of Norah Lange's work.

Emily Licht offered comments on the manuscript during lengthy recitation sessions, Silvia Borzutzky checked the translation with expert eyes, and Danny Talesnik offered key suggestions. Daniel Borzutzky generously offered feedback on the whole book to help make the poems sing.

A research grant from Stanford University made possible collaborations with Susana Lange and a visit to the Biblioteca Sede Oliverio Girondo at Palacio Noel in Buenos Aires. Thanks to the Alice Kaplan Institute for the Humanities at Northwestern University for a publication subvention grant.

The texts of the thirty poems in this volume are based upon the corrected edition found in Oliverio Girondo, *Obra: poesía y prosa* (Buenos Aires: Losada, 2015), along with a careful review of the first editions. We also found it essential to consult the extensive supplement of Girondo criticism collected in Oliverio Girondo, *Obra completa*, ed. Raúl Antelo ([San José]: Universidad de Costa Rica, 1999), and we have elected to follow Antelo's decision to publish a slightly longer variant of the "Open Letter to *La Púa*." All illustrations have been reproduced from the Girondo archives held by the Department of Special Collections of the Hesburgh Libraries of the University of Notre Dame. Special thanks to Sara Weber and Erika Hosselkus.

We are grateful to the editors of the following journals, in which a selection of these translations appeared, sometimes in different form: *Chicago Review*, *Kenyon Review*, *MAKE Magazine*, and *Poetry International*.

Oliverio Girondo (Argentina, 1891-1967) was one of the most important Latin American poets of the twentieth century. He published seven volumes of poetry, including *Twenty Poems to Be Read on the Streetcar, Decalcomania, Scarecrow (Within the Reach of All)*, and *In the Moremarrow*. He was at the center of an Argentine vanguard called the Grupo Florida, which included Jorge Luis Borges, Macedonio Fernández, Xul Solar, and Norah Lange, whom he married.

Harris Feinsod is associate professor of English and Comparative Literature at Northwestern University. He is the author of a literary history, *The Poetry of the Americas: From Good Neighbors to Countercultures*, as well as many essays on modernist literature in Europe and the Americas. He is the director of Open Door Archive. His next book is a cultural history of modernism at sea.

Rachel Galvin is an award-winning poet, translator, and scholar. Her books include two collections of poetry, *Pulleys & Locomotion* and *Elevated Threat Level*; a work of criticism, *News of War: Civilian Poetry 1936-1945*; and *Hitting the Streets*, a translation from the French of Raymond Queneau, which won the Scott Moncrieff Prize for Translation. She is a co-founder of the Outranspo, an international creative translation collective, and assistant professor at the University of Chicago.

OPEN LETTER

Inga Ābele (Latvia)
High Tide
Naja Marie Aidt (Denmark)
Rock, Paper, Scissors
Esther Allen et al. (ed.) (World)
The Man Between: Michael Henry
Heim & a Life in Translation
Bae Suah (South Korea)
A Greater Music
North Station
Svetislav Basara (Serbia)
The Cyclist Conspiracy
Guðbergur Bergsson (Iceland)
Tómas Jónsson, Bestseller
Jean-Marie Blas de Roblès (World)
Island of Point Nemo
Per Aage Brandt (Denmark)
If I Were a Suicide Bomber
Can Xue (China)
Frontier
Vertical Motion
Lúcio Cardoso (Brazil)
Chronicle of the Murdered House
Sergio Chejfec (Argentina)
The Dark
My Two Worlds
The Planets
Eduardo Chirinos (Peru)
The Smoke of Distant Fires
Marguerite Duras (France)
Abahn Sabana David
L'Amour
The Sailor from Gibraltar
Mathias Énard (France)
Street of Thieves
Zone
Macedonio Fernández (Argentina)
The Museum of Eterna's Novel
Rubem Fonseca (Brazil)
The Taker & Other Stories
Rodrigo Fresán (Argentina)
The Bottom of the Sky
The Invented Part
Juan Gelman (Argentina)
Dark Times Filled with Light

Georgi Gospodinov (Bulgaria)
The Physics of Sorrow
Arnon Grunberg (Netherlands)
Tirza
Hubert Haddad (France)
Rochester Knockings:
A Novel of the Fox Sisters
Gail Hareven (Israel)
Lies, First Person
Angel Igov (Bulgaria)
A Short Tale of Shame
Ilya Ilf & Evgeny Petrov (Russia)
The Golden Calf
Zachary Karabashliev (Bulgaria)
18% Gray
Hristo Karastoyanov (Bulgaria)
The Same Night Awaits Us All
Jan Kjærstad (Norway)
The Conqueror
The Discoverer
Josefine Klougart (Denmark)
One of Us Is Sleeping
Carlos Labbé (Chile)
Loquela
Navidad & Matanza
Jakov Lind (Austria)
Ergo
Landscape in Concrete
Andreas Maier (Germany)
Klausen
Lucio Mariani (Italy)
Traces of Time
Amanda Michalopoulou (Greece)
Why I Killed My Best Friend
Valerie Miles (World)
A Thousand Forests in One Acorn:
An Anthology of Spanish-
Language Fiction
Iben Mondrup (Denmark)
Justine
Quim Monzó (Catalonia)
Gasoline
Guadalajara
A Thousand Morons
Elsa Morante (Italy)
Aracoeli

**OPEN
LETTER**

Giulio Mozzi (Italy)
  This Is the Garden
Andrés Neuman (Spain)
  The Things We Don't Do
Jóanes Nielsen (Faroe Islands)
  The Brahmadells
Madame Nielsen (Denmark)
  The Endless Summer
Henrik Nordbrandt (Denmark)
  When We Leave Each Other
Asta Olivia Nordenhof (Denmark)
  The Easiness and the Loneliness
Wojciech Nowicki (Poland)
  Salki
Bragi Ólafsson (Iceland)
  The Ambassador
  Narrator
  The Pets
Kristín Ómarsdóttir (Iceland)
  Children in Reindeer Woods
Diego Trelles Paz (ed.) (World)
  The Future Is Not Ours
Ilja Leonard Pfeijffer (Netherlands)
  Rupert: A Confession
Jerzy Pilch (Poland)
  The Mighty Angel
  My First Suicide
  A Thousand Peaceful Cities
Rein Raud (Estonia)
  The Brother
Mercè Rodoreda (Catalonia)
  Camellia Street
  Death in Spring
  The Selected Stories of Mercè Rodoreda
  War, So Much War
Milen Ruskov (Bulgaria)
  Thrown into Nature
Guillermo Saccomanno (Argentina)
  Gesell Dome
Juan José Saer (Argentina)
  The Clouds
  La Grande
  The One Before
  Scars
  The Sixty-Five Years of Washington

Olga Sedakova (Russia)
  In Praise of Poetry
Mikhail Shishkin (Russia)
  Maidenhair
Sölvi Björn Sigurðsson (Iceland)
  The Last Days of My Mother
Maria José Silveira (Brazil)
  *Her Mother's Mother's Mother and
  Her Daughters*
Andrzej Sosnowski (Poland)
  Lodgings
Albena Stambolova (Bulgaria)
  Everything Happens as It Does
Benjamin Stein (Germany)
  The Canvas
Georgi Tenev (Bulgaria)
  Party Headquarters
Dubravka Ugresic (Europe)
  American Fictionary
  Europe in Sepia
  Fox
  Karaoke Culture
  Nobody's Home
Ludvík Vaculík (Czech Republic)
  The Guinea Pigs
Jorge Volpi (Mexico)
  Season of Ash
Antoine Volodine (France)
  Bardo or Not Bardo
  *Post-Exoticism in Ten Lessons,
  Lesson Eleven*
  Radiant Terminus
Eliot Weinberger (ed.) (World)
  Elsewhere
Ingrid Winterbach (South Africa)
  The Book of Happenstance
  The Elusive Moth
  To Hell with Cronjé
Ror Wolf (Germany)
  Two or Three Years Later
Words Without Borders (ed.) (World)
  The Wall in My Head
Xiao Hong (China)
  Ma Bo'le's Second Life
Alejandro Zambra (Chile)
  The Private Lives of Trees